Bristol VR

John Hypher

Front cover:
Hedingham Omnibuses of Essex still runs a sizeable fleet of VRs, which at its peak numbered over 40 examples. Many are used on schools duties, but some make appearances on stage services. One such appearance was made by L249 (HJB 456W) which is seen at Colchester bus station unloading its passengers in April 2000. This bus started out as Alder Valley 636 in November 1980 and was still in regular use some 20 years later. *John Hypher*

Back cover:
Southern Vectis 682 (FDL 682V) stands spare at Yarmouth bus station during June 2000 and was one of just a handful of closed-top VRs remaining with the company. The following year, however, all that changed and it was converted to open-top and re-registered VDL 744. *John Hypher*

Title page:
Showing off its long wheelbase to advantage is Reading 50 (NRD 50M), one of no fewer than 50 VRTLLs supplied to this municipal fleet, making it the largest customer for these buses. Northern Counties supplied the dual-door bodywork for these buses, which were known locally as 'Jumbos'. This example, seen at Tilehurst in June 1974, was just four months old when photographed. *Martin Curtis*

ACKNOWLEDGEMENTS

I acknowledge with grateful thanks the following people and organisations for their valuable help in the preparation of this book: Roger Barton, David Brown, Stewart J. Brown, Simon Butler, Martin Curtis, Phil Davies, *Haagsche Courant*, Mark Hughes, Graham Jones, Malcolm Keeley, Allan Macfarlane, Iain MacGregor and Geoff Rixon for so readily making their superb collections of VR photographs and slides available to me; also to Michael Bennett, MB Transport Photos and the Bristol Vintage Bus Group, for their photographic contributions, and to the PSV Circle for their kind permission to use material from their publications, in particular the Bristol VR Series Chassis List, which proved to be an invaluable reference, and to *Commercial Motor* magazine for permission to reproduce its VRTSL chassis drawing.

I am indebted to Roger Warwick for allowing me to use material in relation to the '760 Project' from Part 12 of his series of books on United Counties and also for his help and advice concerning its illustration. Thanks are due also to Martin Curtis for saving me time by allowing selected information from the appendices in his book *Bristol VR* (Ian Allan 1994) to be used. My special thanks go to Allan Macfarlane for his ready help during the preparation of this work and for checking the manuscript. His advice, comments and corrections have been invaluable and many of his suggestions have been incorporated in this book.

CONTENTS

First published 2002

ISBN0 7110 2870 2

© John Hypher 2002

Published by Ian Allan Publishing

an imprint of Ian Allan Publishing Ltd, Hersham, Surrey KT12 4RG.
Printed by Ian Allan Printing Ltd, Hersham, Surrey KT12 4RG.

Code: 0209/B1

INTRODUCTION

The glory days of the Bristol VR started in a blaze of publicity more than 35 years ago during the latter part of 1966. Bristol's long-awaited entry into the rear-engined double-deck market was realised when its two prototypes stole the limelight at the 1966 Commercial Motor Show at Earl's Court in September. Indeed, the author was just one of thousands there to climb aboard and to look around these gleaming buses and to savour that unique smell of brand-new vehicles. After much eager anticipation as to what the new VR would actually look like, we were not disappointed. The airy and spacious interiors and the unique and very discreet positioning of their engines presented very favourable impressions which still remain today. These were the beginning of a new era not only for Bristol, but also for the bus industry as a whole.

In those heady days of the 'Sixties and 'Seventies it would have been very difficult to imagine our highways and byways without the ubiquitous Bristol. Yes, of course, models would be updated from time to time and eventually be superseded by others, but depots and bus stations devoid of the sight and sound of the Bristol — never! The same sentiments would also have been equally true of Eastern Coach Works (ECW), which for so many years was synonymous with Bristol double-deckers, saloons and coaches. But alas, the sad reality was that in our fast-changing world both of these long-established and eminent concerns slipped quietly into oblivion during the 'Eighties. But despite that, some 20 years after the last VR was built, examples can still be seen in all-day service as well as on school runs and as open-toppers on both coastal and inland sightseeing services. This achievement in itself is a testimony to the robustness and sound engineering associated with these buses. The reality, however, is that by the end of this decade the only Bristol vehicles around will be those in the hands of preservationists. Some of these will no doubt be proud to give their VRs a summer airing to the rally fields to give us a nostalgic glimpse of these fine vehicles, and for a few hours to re-live those glory days once again.

The Bristol marque has been plying our streets for close on a century. It was 1907 when the Bristol Tramways & Carriage Co decided to build its own chassis. These were constructed initially for its own use but were soon made available to other operators as their reputation for reliability spread throughout the industry. It could be said that the VR's ancestry stretches back to the handful of double-deck-bodied examples of the very basic 4-ton chassis of the early 1920s. The 1925 Commercial Motor Show saw Bristol unveil its new A-type chassis, which at the same time heralded the introduction of Bristol's chassis type letters. The A remained in production until 1928 and a number received double-deck bodies. It was the G-type, however, introduced in 1931, which really put Bristol double-deckers on the map, and three years later these were sold as oil-engined chassis featuring Gardner 5LW power-units. They had rather imposing high radiators, bonnets and dumb irons which helped to give them an altogether solid appearance. It can also be said that it was these vehicles, in double-deck terms at least, that introduced the familiar 'Bristol look'. This characteristic was continued with the K-type, which came on stream a couple of years before the war, in 1937. The K continued to be produced for some 20 years, and during that time over 4,000 were built. 1945 saw the introduction of the lower PV2 radiator and bonnet which certainly enhanced the appearance of these vehicles and continued that unique 'Bristol look'. Over its 20-year production run the K underwent a number of changes, both in terms of length and width, to reflect new legislation, and also in terms of wider engine choice. Initially the K was 26ft long and 7ft 6in wide, but from 1950 the permissible length was increased to 27ft and the width to 8ft. Accordingly a longer version, the KS, was produced together with a longer and wider chassis, the KSW. When introduced, the K was available only with a Gardner 5LW engine (K5G), but as production continued and the K 'family' grew, the choice eventually included the Gardner 6LW (K6G), Bristol AVW (K6B) and AEC 470 (K6A) engines.

While the K-type was still in full swing and operators were busy re-equipping with new buses after the war, a completely new concept was being developed by Bristol, namely the Lodekka. The first of two Bristol-engined prototypes was built in 1949, and these unusual-looking vehicles, with their low floors, large wide radiators and chrome bumpers, were thoroughly tested before a batch of pre-production LD models entered service during 1953. At just 13ft 4in high, these revolutionary new buses were built to lowbridge dimensions but without the sunken gangway upstairs and its consequent intrusion into the offside lower-deck. Indeed, apart from providing standards of passenger comfort on both decks associated with highbridge buses, they were low enough to make them completely versatile in all double-deck fleets. Production Lodekkas came on stream during 1954 and a small batch of half a dozen 30ft LDLs was produced in 1957. When both the pre-production and production LDs appeared, they had lost the traditional bonnet and the polished metal radiators and bumpers of the prototypes. Instead, they had a wide engine cowl featuring a full-depth outline slatted dummy radiator grille which allowed air to flow to the concealed radiator behind. Later LDs had a slightly modified cowl, which also featured a shorter radiator grille and shorter mudguards which served to lighten their front-end appearance. During 1962 the cowl was further modified and incorporated a new 'tubular' surround to the grille, which for the first time included the type name *Lodekka* on its lower edge.

During 1958 two flat-floor prototypes were built which eliminated the need for sunken lower-deck gangways. At 27ft and 30ft long, these were the forerunners of the FS and FL types respectively. In 1959 eight pre-production flat-floor chassis, designated LDS, were built, together with the prototype FLF, the first forward-entrance Lodekka. Production of the new flat-floor Lodekkas, comprising the FS, FL, FSF and FLF commenced during 1960, and options for power units in the Lodekka range comprised engines from Gardner, Bristol, and (later) Leyland.

Just as Leyland and AEC buses had their own distinctive sounds, so Bristols produced their own melodic sound effects. Five- and six-cylinder Ks were easily distinguishable from one another, as were five- and six-cylinder Lodekkas, within the overall 'Bristol sound'. Unlike the K-type, the sounds from a five-cylinder Lodekka never seemed to cut the mustard and seemed somewhat flat, whereas the multi-pitched music from a semi-automatic FLF totally reflected its lively performance and remains unique among bus sounds.

A small quantity of lengthened FLFs was built for the Scottish Bus Group and the Tilling Group's Eastern National towards the end of Lodekka production; these were 1ft longer than normal and could readily be distinguished from the standard 30ft vehicles by their longer rearmost side windows. Over 5,200 Lodekkas were produced, with the last examples — all FLFs — being delivered in September 1968. These ubiquitous vehicles were gradually superseded by the VR together with new working practices which now extended one-man operation to include double-deckers. Generous enticements were offered to operators in the shape of bus grants for approved new rear-engined vehicles to help this process along.

Despite the enticements offered to operators, the VRT took a while to establish itself and was ordered initially in relatively small numbers. This may have been because it was untried and untested and as such was too much of an unknown quantity for operators to plunge in with large orders for a vehicle straight from the drawing-board.

The author spent a significant part of his career in the bus industry surrounded by Bristol buses, including the K, L, LS, MW, SU, Lodekka, RE, LH and VR types, and has built up a wealth of knowledge and a fondness for these trusty and familiar workhorses. This book tells the story in words and pictures of the very last double-deckers to come from Brislington bearing the Bristol badge. It is a colourful story which aims to capture the spirit and diversity of a bus built to survive — despite a shaky start!

The trusty front-engined Lodekka had a production run of 15 years from 1953 to 1968 and was superseded by the rear-engined Bristol VR, which remained in production from 1968 to 1981. Seen at Bournemouth in the summer of 1964 is brand-new Southern National FLF6B 2050 (ATA 119B) on the Weymouth service, which was run jointly with Hants & Dorset. Note the white steering wheel, which was a feature of Southern and Western National Bristols for many years. *John Hypher*

1. THE NEW ORDER

While Bristol was supplying its underfloor-engined single-deck buses and coaches and its F-series front-engined double-deck Lodekkas, it was busy developing its first rear-engined chassis. First to be completed was the prototype RELL single-deck bus, which was introduced during 1962 and featured an underslung Gardner 6HLX engine. Its appearance was very modern and airy, featuring deep individual wrap-round windscreens and an attractive new design of radiator grille built into a stylish front panel, with rounded sides to follow the curvature of the windscreen. As a matter of personal preference, the author has always considered that the prototype and early production RE buses which followed similar styling looked more attractive than subsequent ECW design changes to these buses. Despite being rear-engined, the underslung engine position allowed the emergency door to be sited at the extreme rear of these buses at the end of the

sloping centre gangway. This was, yet again, certainly a piece of neat design work on the part of Bristol and ECW. The RELL was followed in 1963 by the prototype high-framed RELH coach. Similarities in body style with contemporary MW coaches were immediately apparent, but a new feature was the 'tubular'-style Lodekka grille featuring 'ECW' on its lower edge. Remarkably, the RELH had a traditional boot at the rear, and to the untrained eye could have passed as a normal-layout underfloor-engined coach! Both the RELL and RELH were 36ft long, but from 1967 shorter-wheelbase RESL and RESH versions also became available. Yet another RE model was introduced in 1969 in the shape of the REMH extra-long-wheelbase coach chassis, which when bodied was 39ft 4in long and used on long-distance motorway services. Operators ordered the REs in large quantities for both bus and coach work, and Bristol had certainly found a winner not only with

Bristol's first rear-engined chassis was introduced in 1962. This was a 36ft single-decker with its engine located beneath the chassis frame behind the rear axle. Production of the RE series began at the end of the following year, and this photograph shows 1203 (AFE 473B), an early (1964) RELL in the Lincolnshire Road Car fleet. Another couple of years would elapse before Bristol's rear-engined double-decker was unveiled.
John Hypher

GGM 431D, the first VR prototype (chassis VRX001) shows off its elegant and well-proportioned lines in this official photograph. It was launched at the 1966 Commercial Motor Show at Earls Court in September together with the second prototype, HHW 933D. Although owned by Bristol Commercial Vehicles, it was finished in the red and cream livery of Central SMT, in which fleet it was trialled. The VR was developed as the N-type, and this designation remained as part of its Central SMT fleet number — BN331. *ECW*

its traditional Tilling Group customers but also with BET and municipal operators. Significant orders were also placed by Citybus and Ulsterbus in Northern Ireland which managed to persuade British Leyland to supply these chassis for several years after production had officially ceased.

Both Gardner and Leyland engines were available in their 6HLW/6HLX or O.600/O.680 versions respectively. Indeed, it was the REs that introduced the familiar 'Bristol whine' to our streets, a sound perpetuated by Bristol rear-engined buses and which in its own way became as familiar as the unique sound of the Lodekka. It is appropriate at this stage to mention that Bristol chassis and ECW bodies had not been available to operators outside the State sector since nationalisation of the Tilling Group in 1948. Both Bristol and ECW were thus unable to accept any orders from outside customers until 1965, when the Government invited Leyland to take a 25% shareholding in these concerns and at the same time made their products freely available once again on the open market. Between these dates nearly all Bristol passenger vehicles had been automatically bodied by ECW. Despite this embargo, however,

an interesting vehicle being supplied primarily to municipal and BET fleets during the 'Fifties and 'Sixties was the front-engined Dennis Loline which mirrored the Lodekka and was built under licence from Bristol, thereby effectively making their revolutionary Lodekka available to fleets outside the State sector! With its RE range, Bristol certainly had the edge in terms of production and popularity and far outstripped the rear-engined single-deck offerings from AEC, Daimler and Leyland. From 1965 with the new freedom of the open market, the RE could be bodied by any coachbuilder and this enabled operators to order from their usual or preferred coachbuilders if they so chose.

Production of the rear-engined Leyland Atlantean double-decker started in 1958, and this was followed in 1960 by the introduction of the Daimler Fleetline. Unlike the Bristol RE, these had the engine mounted vertically across the back of the chassis and normally enclosed within a separate 'bustle' to the rear of the lower-deck coachwork. Both models were very well established by the time the VR was launched in 1966 and had been supplied in some quantity to municipal and BET fleets in particular. Early production of the Atlantean and Fleetline ran happily alongside the mainstream front-engined double-deckers from both Leyland and Daimler, in the shape of Leyland's Titan range and Daimler's CV series, as well as the popular Regent V from AEC. The decision either to re-order the traditional front-engined chassis or opt for the new rear engines depended on operator preference and whether the higher seating capacities of 77/78 and modernity of the rear-engined buses were regarded as important. At this stage, however, the State sector had no such choice.

Bristol was going down a very different avenue with the development of its rear-engined double-decker, encompassing a far broader and a more far-reaching approach than the design and production of just another chassis to compete with those available from Leyland and Daimler. Bristol's was a conceptual approach which it saw as revolutionising the whole question of supply to meet not only the traditional needs of operators but also flexible enough to meet any future needs and trends. This would give operators not only a new rear-engined double-decker but also a high-capacity single-decker, as well as coaches, within the same standardised chassis range. By placing the engine longitudinally on the offside of the vehicle, behind the rear axle, they could achieve all this

and offer a flat floor throughout the vehicle. Indeed, this provision of a flat and low floor continued the theme introduced so successfully with the Lodekka. The first handful of chassis to be built, known initially as the N-type, were produced with high hopes that this concept would capture the imagination of the industry and take a significant market share of both single- and double-deck markets. Two of these prototype chassis were given virtually identical ECW double-deck bodies and were presented to the industry at the 1966 Commercial Motor Show. To be at the show at all was a significant landmark for Bristol and ECW, as under State ownership neither had been permitted to show (let alone sell) their wares to a wider audience. Between being built and launched, their chassis designation was changed from N to the more familiar VR, which stood for Vertical Rear, the position of its engine. The chassis were given smart, well-proportioned ECW bodies of traditional appearance and featuring a front entrance/exit, but these buses could equally accommodate centre doors and/or rear doors behind the rear axle. Large-capacity single-deckers with any combination of entry and alighting points were also possible, and it is perhaps a pity that one of the prototype chassis was not bodied as a saloon to show off this potential.

HHW 933D, the second prototype VR (chassis VRX002), was painted in Tilling green and cream livery. It was put through its paces in the Mansfield area with Mansfield District Traction but remained in the ownership of Bristol Commercial Vehicles for the duration of the trials. This view highlights the long rear overhang necessary to accommodate the longitudinal engine. Notice (in both this and the previous photograph) how well-hidden the engine is. These buses could easily be mistaken for underfloor-engined models! *ECW*

2. INTO TRAFFIC — THE VRL

The two prototypes, designated VRX, remained unique, but had similar chassis gone into production alongside VRTs these would have been classified VRLSL6G. Both prototypes entered service with State-owned operators, one (GGM 431D) with Central SMT — part of the Scottish Bus Group — in a deep red livery and the other (HHW 933D) with Mansfield District Traction in Tilling green. GGM 431D featured SBG's standard trapezoid style of destination display, while HHW 933D was finished to Bristol Omnibus Co specification as seen by its destination equipment and the exclusive use of sliding window vents. Powered by 10.45-litre Gardner 6LX engines, they measured 33ft long and 13ft 8in high. Seating was provided for 45 passengers on the upper deck and 35 on the lower. Several Tilling Group companies were visited by the green prototype for demonstration purposes, and it also ventured across the Channel to the French town of Metz, where it ran during British Shopping Week early in 1967.

As might be expected with a brand-new design of vehicle, both prototypes experienced their fair share of teething troubles and spent lengthy periods out of service awaiting remedial attention and modifications. Scotland was rather a long way to travel to see the red prototype in action (or possibly not!) but the author did make various pilgrimages to see the impressive green prototype (both on and off the road) in Mansfield. A major part of the course for prototypes is to run them under normal service conditions and to identify any problem areas and design weaknesses and to find solutions to satisfactorily overcome them. This whole shakedown process is valuable to builder and to operators alike, as the more problems that can be sorted out at this stage makes for a much more reliable design when full production starts. Naturally, Bristol wanted another quality product to supersede the Lodekka and to continue its hitherto excellent reputation within the industry.

Just like the two prototype Lodekkas, these VRs remained the only examples of their kind for a while, and more than two years were to elapse before the next VRL made its appearance

at the end of 1968. This was like nothing seen before and came in the shape of a very sleek and stylish 36ft VRLLH6L double-deck coach for Ribble subsidiary W. C. Standerwick of Blackpool. At this time, Standerwick was running an impressive fleet of Leyland Atlantean double-deck coaches between Lancashire and London known as 'Gay Hostesses', but this new cream- and red-liveried 60-seat ECW-bodied VR took design into another dimension. Gone was the bus-derived bodyshell with coach seats, in favour of a completely new and exciting design specifically tailored for coach travel. One of the main problems with the Atlantean coaches had been the lack of forward visibility for passengers on the lower deck. On the nearside, the mini-bulkhead behind the doors caused a partial obstruction, but far worse was the zero forward visibility, caused by the staircase, for passengers travelling on the offside. The new high-framed VRL solved that entirely by having its entry/exit point located behind the nearside seating area and the staircase positioned opposite the entrance on the offside, again behind the passenger seats. Generous luggage space and a toilet were also provided in their own dedicated but easily accessible area at the rear of the coach, alleviating the need for passengers and luggage to travel together in the main saloon area; racks for light hand luggage continued to be sited above the seats on both decks in the usual way.

Fitted with a Leyland O.680 engine, the first VRL coach was to remain unique for a couple of years while it was thoroughly tested, much of it in motorway service to and from London, after which delivery commenced of a further 29 slightly modified but generally similar (Series 2) vehicles. The author well remembers regularly seeing these fine coaches at Victoria Coach Station not only dwarfing everything else there but upstaging them too, with their modern yet elegant appearance.

The only other VRLs built were 14 similar chassis for Johannesburg during 1969 and 11 for Pretoria in 1970/1. These too were large 36ft double-deckers and were bodied by Bus Bodies (South Africa) for use as service buses. They featured twin staircases and doors ahead of the front axle and also

Prototype HHW 933D, complete with 'On Hire' label in its left-hand windscreen but minus its front panel, is pictured while taking time out for repairs at Mansfield depot during 1967. *John Hypher*

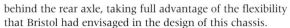

behind the rear axle, taking full advantage of the flexibility that Bristol had envisaged in the design of this chassis.

Meanwhile, the British bus industry was embarking upon another period of change. The operation of one-man double-deckers had been legalised during 1966, and to encourage disposal of older crew-operated buses in favour of new one-man operated vehicles, generous bus grants were made available towards their purchase. In the grand plan of things, it emerged that the only double-deck chassis that qualified for bus grant were those with engines mounted transversely at the

rear. Sadly, this sounded the death knell for the longitudinally-engined VRL as far as the domestic bus market was concerned. Coaches *per se* were not eligible for bus grant, although by designating them as dual-purpose, fitting fare-collection equipment and then fulfilling specified minimum requirements in terms of stage-carrriage mileage, operators could still qualify for assistance within the scheme. Even this was of no help to Bristol with its VRL, however. To maintain a presence in the domestic double-deck market, Bristol's only option was to turn the engine through 90° and start again. Thus the transverse-engined VRT, instead of being an option within the VR range for operators with a preference for this layout, was now thrust forward, untested and ahead of schedule, as Bristol's primary double-deck chassis. As a consequence, much of the in-service testing and shaking-down of the two prototypes was of limited use for what was

effectively a brand-new design involving new engineering — something with which Bristol's red-face department would soon have to deal. With the bus grant carrot being dangled in front of them, there was no way that operators would order the VRL at full price for bus work in anything other than penny numbers, so for Bristol to continue with this model as its primary double-deck chassis was not an option. It is interesting to speculate, however, just how this revolutionary design would have fared against the Atlantean and Fleetline, had it qualified for bus grant.

With no further orders received for the revolutionary VRL, production came to an end, after 55 chassis had been built, with construction of the last vehicles of the Standerwick order (delivered during the summer of 1972), thereby ending Bristol's dream of a versatile range of offside-rear-engined buses and coaches.

3. PIT STOP — THE VRT

No prototypes of the transverse-engined VRs were ever built. Instead, Bristol went straight into production, with a long-wheelbase VRTLL model. Scottish Omnibuses was the very first customer and took delivery of 25 of these 83-seat buses during the latter part of 1968. But it very soon became apparent to SOL that the purchase of these vehicles was a big mistake. Their lack of reliability in service, together with multitudinous problems also experienced with the short-wheelbase VRTSL buses purchased subsequently, and similar reports coming from other Scottish Bus Group (SBG) companies, culminated in their mass withdrawal and disposal during the early 1970s. Even after the teething problems had been largely sorted out with the Series 2 buses and with the proven reliability of the Series 3 VRs, the damage had been done, and SBG would never again turn to Bristol for new double-deckers. SBG's faith in the trusty Lodekka remained undented, however, and a deal was struck whereby most of the SBG VRs were exchanged for the newest Lodekkas from a number of National Bus Company fleets (see Appendix I). Their new owners eventually brought the former Scottish VRTs up to standard by incorporating modifications and improved components which were now available to transform these rejects into more reliable buses. This is something which arguably SBG could have done itself, but by now it had lost confidence in the VR and decided to rid itself of these troublesome buses. Indeed, the author well remembers some of these buses arriving at Eastern Counties' central works in Norwich looking very sorry for themselves, and after several weeks of work being spent on them eventually leaving there ready for service resplendent in a gleaming coat of poppy-red paint after a thorough overhaul. It could be argued that the wholesale and well-publicised rejection of the VR from the Scottish Bus Group had a considerable adverse effect on the type's short- and medium-term reputation. Rear-engined chassis from other manufacturers also fell well short of the mark in terms of reliability, some more than others, but did not bring about such an extreme or public reaction from their owners.

The author had an opportunity to drive some ex-SBG VRs while at Eastern Counties, and the only adverse comments about both these and Series 1 vehicles in general concerned the heavy throttle and a lumbering and sluggish pull-away from a standing start. (The Series 2 VRs were altogether more responsive by comparison and were kinder to the knees and ankles, as well as to motorists courteous enough to flash you out of bus stops and rightfully expecting a prompt exit!)

Meanwhile, south of the border, former Tilling Group companies had started taking delivery of their first VRs — all short-wheelbase VRTSLs — from January 1969. Among the first of these were some for Western National, which the author and photograph contributor Phil Davies saw earning their keep in Plymouth soon after delivery. On first impression they compared very favourably with the Atlanteans that plied the city for the Corporation. Their classic body design, stylish front end, fully-enclosed engine area and cream window rubbers showed ECW at its best.

These Series 1 buses differed noticeably in several respects from the prototypes, not least because the lower-deck windows did not extend to the very rear, owing to the transverse engine. For the same reason, the pair of lower-deck back windows of the prototypes, the nearside of which had comprised part of the emergency exit, were now replaced by a single shallow window above the engine casing. The emergency door was re-sited to a new position behind the offside rear wheel, and another noticeable difference was the windscreen arrangement, which no longer consisted of two separate windows but instead featured a split screen with a polished-metal centre support. While this list of differences is in no way intended to be exhaustive, the other main noticeable feature was the shorter rear overhang made possible by the transverse engine.

Overall, striking similarities with the FLF Lodekka were readily apparent both inside and out, particularly on the upper deck and also along the lower-deck window areas. This was because ECW had decided to incorporate a number of body

◀ Western National was among the first operators to receive the new VRT, with 10 entering service during the first few months of 1969. Fresh out of the paintshops in gleaming leaf green and white is the last of that batch, 1059 (OTA 293G), seen in Plymouth during August 1980. *Geoff Rixon*

features from the Lodekka into its VR design, rather than completely re-style the body, and thus perpetuated that distinctive 'ECW look'.

With the exception of the last 10 chassis, all Series 1 VRTs, which comprised 25 VRTLL and 237 VRTSL vehicles, featured flat windscreens and front entrance / exits. Each was bodied by ECW and powered by a Gardner six-cylinder engine.

The last 10 chassis were built for Stockport Corporation but were unfortunately destroyed by fire at East Lancs. Happily though, it was possible to salvage one of these chassis, which was later exported to Australia; it was given a Smithfield twin-door 47-seat single-deck body in 1973 and remains the only VR ever completed as a single-decker. Despite the relaxation in availability of Bristol buses, all but the 10 ill-fated Stockport chassis were built for operators within the State sector. It is interesting to note, however, that Stockport Corporation,

Pictured at York station in November 1977 is York-West Yorkshire 3922 (YWR 204G). This bus started life in March 1969 as West Yorkshire VR22 before joining the York fleet. The notice in the left-hand windscreen advises passengers that they must have the right money ready for the farebox. Notice also the 'T'-shape destination/number display.
Martin Curtis

Eastern Counties VR371 (TNG 371G), new in May 1969, has lost its original Tilling red and cream livery in favour of NBC's corporate poppy red and white. It still carries pay-as-you-enter transfers rather than the small illuminated signs which became standard fitments.
John Hypher collection

formerly a dedicated Leyland customer, chose the Bristol VRT for its first rear-engined double-deckers, and in so doing became the VR's first municipal customer.

Tilling and SBG companies took the first few, and the newly formed National Bus Company (NBC) took the rest. NBC was formed under the 1968 Transport Act and amalgamated the former Tilling companies and British Electric Traction (BET) companies into a unified organisation from 1 January 1969.

Companies purchasing Series 1 buses were:

Alexander (Midland)
Brighton, Hove & District
Central SMT
Eastern Counties
Eastern National
Lincolnshire
Midland General
Scottish Omnibuses
Southern Vectis
Thames Valley
United Auto
United Counties
West Yorkshire (including Keighley and York)
Western National
Western SMT

Liveries carried by Tilling Group buses were generally Tilling-standard red or green, relieved by one cream band, but there were some interesting exceptions to this, which continued to be carried by early VRs for a while. Control of Brighton, Hove & District had passed to Southdown after the formation of NBC, but happily the VRs on order were delivered in BH&D's distinctive and attractive livery of red and cream. Midland General's VRs carried that company's attractive blue and cream livery.

It is no secret that the Series 1 VRTs with English operators also had a chequered early career, with levels of unreliability and failure rates never previously associated with Bristol vehicles. Both bus companies and Bristol engineers worked tirelessly to overcome these problems, but it was an uphill task because all these buses were effectively untried, untested and unproven prototypes, throwing up a myriad of problems, the causes of which needed to be identified and remedied with suitable modifications on a fleet basis. This called for a great deal of co-operation on both sides, and this eventually paid off. Many of the problems centred around the transmission, but overheating and engine-compartment fires were also a major cause for concern. Going straight into production was a make-or-break decision which could so easily have ended in disaster for the company by irrevocably destroying its reputation and standing in the manufacturing industry. But it was a battle the company was determined to win, and eventually win it did, with a superb and reliable bus which became widely acclaimed and which was vindicated by the volume of orders and quantities built.

New to Thames Valley in May 1969 as its 504, UBL 245G is seen at Victoria Coach Station bearing new number 905 and Alder Valley fleetnames following the amalgamation of Aldershot & District and Thames Valley by the newly formed National Bus Company. Passengers are boarding ready for the return trip to Reading on service B. *John Hypher*

No fewer than 252 Series 1 VRTs were built for service with State-owned operators, among which was United Counties. Dating from October 1969, 757 (UBD 757H) is seen on its way to Bedford, bearing unmistakable evidence of its ownership! *John Hypher collection*

15

4. TURNING THE CORNER — SERIES 2

When the Series 2 VRs were introduced in 1970, there was very little visually to tell them apart from their predecessors. Externally the changes were subtle. The only sure way of knowing whether you were looking at a Series 1 or 2 VR was to check the offside of the bus and see where the rearmost drainage outlet was between decks. ECW had moved it forward slightly, from being over the small window ahead of the emergency door to a new position over the next normal-size window. In addition, poor ventilation and some engine-compartment fires on Series 1 buses prompted a modified engine-cover assembly incorporating large side grilles to supplement and improve upon the two small apertures on the rear cover. However, because these grilles were introduced retrospectively on earlier buses, it was not always possible to tell at a glance whether a bus was a Series 1 or a Series 2.

What had originally started as a one-piece engine cover had now given way to a more practical three-piece assembly, with separately hinged side panels and rear centre panel. To assist cooling still further, a fan now featured under the bonnet, behind the nearside grille, and significantly greater mechanical reliability was achieved by incorporating modified transmission components, in place of those which clearly had not been up to the job and had let the original buses down.

Unlike their predecessors, which were instantly recognisable and were very much standardised buses, Series 2 VRs came in various guises, bearing the bodywork of three additional coachbuilders. Even ECW later extended its range with three heights to choose from — ultra-low, standard and full-height — as well as coach-seated and twin-door options. Until one got used to the idea that, from now on, all VRs didn't look the same, it was a little disconcerting to be in a strange town and to hear a VR complete with Bristol whine, but see a bus that looked nothing like a VR! Not only were there new shapes to get used to but new customers also, together with their spectrum of liveries. NBC, as expected, led the order book, but municipal and PTE operators placed some significant orders too. The first of a handful of independent

operators to order the VR was Hutchings & Cornelius of South Petherton in Somerset, which took delivery of an attractively liveried brown and cream example. As might reasonably be expected, customers which ordered buses did so to carry passengers, but one notable exception was an order for one bus from the Department of the Environment which required its VR not to carry passengers but to put trainee PSV driving examiners through their paces! This vehicle was based at Cardington in Bedfordshire. Most of the Series 2 build comprised standard-wheelbase low-framed buses, but over 90 long-wheelbase examples were also produced, many of which, unusually, featured high frames.

Long-established coachbuilders Northern Counties, East Lancs and Metro-Cammell-Weymann (MCW) were selected to provide the bodywork on Series 2 chassis for Gelligaer UDC, Reading Corporation, Sheffield Transport, Merseyside PTE and West Midlands PTE. Some of these styled their bodies in much the same way as for Atlanteans and Fleetlines, in that they didn't incorporate the engine compartment within the bodywork, but rather left the engine as a separate 'bustle' on the back of the frame. Northern Counties, however, which produced the bodies for the Gelligaer and Reading fleets, enclosed the engine areas much as ECW did. Gelligaer called for just a trio of buses, whereas the much larger Reading ordered some 31 long-wheelbase VRs, featuring centre exits which were gaining a popular following. The size and squareness of these buses earned them the nickname of 'Jumbos' locally.

East Lancs was the chosen coachbuilder of both Sheffield Transport and Merseyside PTE, although the latter's initial order had been placed by Liverpool Corporation before being absorbed into the PTE. All these buses featured a rear engine 'bustle'. Before placing its order for 50 conventional standard-wheelbase front-entrance buses, Merseyside received 59 twin-door, long-wheelbase, high-framed VRTLHs. There should have been a further bus, bringing the total to 60, but this was destroyed in the fire at the East Lancs factory. Sheffield's 18 buses had front entrances and were later absorbed into the South Yorkshire PTE fleet. West Midlands PTE had the unique distinction of running the only VRs to be bodied by MCW; 200 front-entrance buses were bodied locally, and these too featured rear engine 'bustles'.

As already mentioned, dual-door buses were very much in vogue, particularly for use on urban services, and ECW supplied these to Southdown, Bristol Omnibus and Northern General. These buses also had centre staircases with forward-ascending stairs, and this meant that the seating arrangements on both decks had to be re-configured accordingly. From the offside, these buses were easily recognisable through having the solid staircase panel halfway along the lower deck instead of immediately aft of the driver's cab. Another option, specified for inter-urban use, was the coach-seated version supplied to City of Oxford and to Alder Valley for use on their respective London services. These vehicles were generally supplied in small quantities, just 11 Series 2 VRTs being so equipped.

By now the VR was finding its feet and was becoming a very versatile and ubiquitous vehicle throughout England and, to a lesser extent, Wales, although in fairness their numbers within the principality were on the increase too. (After the VR/Lodekka exchanges between the SBG and NBC, only Scotland, within mainland Britain, remained without any VRs for several years, until 1977 when Tayside received 25 long-wheelbase Series 3 VRTs bodied by Alexander.) Coach-seated VRTs and VRLs were regular visitors to Victoria Coach Station on timetabled services from Oxford, Reading and the North West, having replaced coaches, Lodekkas and Atlanteans. At the same time, VRs were also to be found on all kinds of services, ranging from those in rural Cornwall and Norfolk through to the high-density city services in Birmingham, Bristol and Liverpool, which saw them in front-line action seven days a week. And throughout the rest of the country they became a familiar sight on a vast network of inter-urban routes.

The early 'Seventies witnessed a major period of change throughout a significant part of the industry. Former Tilling and BET companies were going through a process of integration under the newly formed National Bus Company,

which involved a measure of reorganisation and the introduction of a new corporate livery. Under the 1968 Transport Act, part of the municipal sector also was being reorganised and amalgamated into large Passenger Transport Executives in the major urban areas, with all those involved losing their previous local identities and independence. Sadly many of their old-established and distinctive liveries went too.

The same 'corporatisation' was happening also as National Bus policies were implemented. The old and well-established variety of liveries, particularly of the colourful former BET companies, gave way to leaf green or poppy red, while all NBC coaches were painted all-over white. East Midland, East Yorkshire, Devon General, City of Oxford, Ribble and Southdown were fortunate in having their early VRs delivered in their traditional BET liveries, which they happily retained for a short while before turning to poppy red or leaf green. Of the PTEs, SELNEC, which covered Greater Manchester, was the

▲ Squeaky-clean after driving through the bus wash is Lincolnshire Road Car Series 2 VRT 1907 (LFE 141H) in Tilling green and cream livery. Note the steam coming from both front and rear wheels!
Michael Bennett

Newcastle-upon-Tyne provides the backdrop for United Auto Series 2 VRT 629 (DHN 229H), photographed when just two years old in August 1972. United eventually built up a fleet of more than 200 VRTSLs over the 12 years the type was in production. *BaMMOT collection*

The first VRs to be bodied by Northern Counties were three supplied to the then Gelligaer UDC municipal fleet in April 1971. Previously numbered 41, the last of the trio, by now numbered 55 (BTX 541J), is seen 10 years later in the livery of Rhymney Valley District Council, which assumed control of the fleets of Gelligaer, Caerphilly and Bedwas & Machen during 1974 as part of local-government reorganisation. *Malcolm Keeley*

most radical in its choice of orange and white. Its fleet incorporated the former Manchester City Transport undertaking, together with a number of surrounding municipal operators and part of the North Western Road Car Co, whose ordered VRs were delivered from ECW to SELNEC in the bright new livery.

It will be recalled that cream window rubbers were introduced by ECW during production of F-series Lodekkas and this practice continued with the VR prototypes and the majority of earlier production buses. During the Tilling era, the cream surrounds very tastefully complemented the areas of cream within the group liveries, but the new NBC corporate livery replaced the cream waistbands with white and featured light grey wheels. Accordingly, ECW was asked to change the colour of the window rubbers to grey, to co-ordinate with the new image being introduced across the group.

During the latter months of 1972, ECW gave its VR bus body design a makeover which totally transformed and modernised its front-end appearance and set the scene for all future deliveries. The flat front gave way to a new double-curvature two-piece windscreen, with central rubber support, and a re-styled and rounded front cowl and grille moulding. The windscreen itself was deeper, this being reflected by the band across the top of the screen being noticeably shallower than before.

This very pleasing modernisation was not all that the ECW designers had come up with. They were well aware that, as operators needed to replace older vehicles and looked around for suitable alternatives, operating conditions and traditional preference dictated the need for a number of variations to be available to make the VR an attractive replacement in their fleets. Standardisation played a part too, and if ECW could provide bodywork to meet several needs within a fleet this would encourage operators to stay loyal. Accordingly, it introduced ultra-low bodies and also a full-height version. Ultra-low bodies were supplied particularly to operators where low bridges and height restrictions meant that vehicle height was critical for safe passage along a particular route or routes. Potteries and Yorkshire Traction, for instance, specified these bodies for all of their Series 2 VRs to give operating flexibility in difficult areas and to reduce the possibility of mistakes being made when allocating vehicles. The 3in difference between these and standard-height bodies was achieved by fitting decambered springs and adopting a slightly sunken gangway on the lower deck. In the manner pioneered by the Lodekka, it was thus possible to produce a highbridge-layout bus to lowbridge dimensions and maintain passenger comfort throughout. Externally, these buses could be spotted by the complete elimination of the white band over the windscreen, due to the height reduction. As offending bridges and other

▲ Three NBC operators ordered dual-door bodywork from ECW for their Series 2 VRTs. Wearing its attractive green and cream one-man livery is Bristol Omnibus C5007 (EHU 366K), used on Bristol City services from new in July 1972. Southdown and Northern General were the other companies which specified this layout for their buses. *Phil Davies collection*

The Series 2 really saw the VR come into its own in many ways. City of Oxford was the first company to receive coach-seated VRTs and among the first to operate ECW's ultra-lowheight coachwork, as depicted by 105 (NUD 105L). Looking smart in NBC dual-purpose livery, this coach was one of nine similar vehicles in this fleet and was new in March 1973. It was captured on film at Oxford's Gloucester Green bus station in October 1975. *Martin Curtis*

obstructions were gradually removed in later years, some companies were able to relax their stringent requirements and operate standard-height buses. Other customers taking delivery of these ultra-low bodies were Alder Valley, City of Oxford, Cumberland, Maidstone & District and United Counties.

Towards the end of Series 2 production in 1975, the first of the ECW full-height buses were supplied to Maidstone & District, which thus gained the unique distinction of running ultra-low, standard and full-height ECW-bodied VRs. In terms of height, the full-height bodies were generally comparable with those being supplied by Northern Counties,

East Lancs and MCW and, at 10in higher than the standard ECW body, were made available to operators which preferred traditional highbridge dimensions with extra lower-saloon headroom. From the front, these buses could be recognised by a deep band above the windscreen and, from the rear, by their deeper lower-deck rear window.

A grand total of 1,160 Series 2 VRT chassis was produced, consisting of 1,069 VRTSL, 60 VRTLH and 31 VRTLL, and each was powered by a Gardner engine. Bodywork was supplied by ECW (798), East Lancs (128), Northern Counties (34) and MCW (200), to the following customers:

The first VR to enter service with Hants & Dorset was Series 2, 1304 (CRU 304L) in December 1972. Its sisters CRU 301-3/5/6L came on stream the following month bearing fleetnumbers 3301-3/5/6. This rare photo of CRU 304L carrying its very short-lived number was taken at Poole bus station when brand new, just days before being renumbered 3304.
Phil Davies

The bus industry has always derived additional income from selling space on its buses to advertisers. During the 1970s bus advertising entered a new dimension, with entire buses being painted as mobile hoardings for a whole variety of organisations. A myriad of colours and designs started to be seen on buses right across the country, with a wide range of concepts appearing in paint ranging from the bland to the brilliant, depending on one's point of view. The fee charged for this service included the cost of repaint back into fleet colours at the end of the contract. Potteries Series 2 VRT 618 (REH 818M), with ECW ultra-low bodywork, is seen at Stafford bus station in May 1976 bearing a red, white and blue advertisement for the Britannia Building Society.
Martin Curtis

Brand-new Hants & Dorset 3310 (NRU 310M) is seen picking up passengers in Southampton in February 1974. The Hants & Dorset fleet used to be painted Tilling green and cream, but under NBC ownership this was changed to poppy red and white, as worn by this bus. On the Series 2 Bristol changed its original one-piece engine cover to a more practical three-piece assembly with improved ventilation, as clearly shown in this view. *Phil Davies*

West Midlands PTE 4649 (GOG 649N) shows off its rear engine bustle in Birmingham during July 1977. VRs featuring bustles were relatively few in number and were supplied only by MCW and East Lancs. West Midlands VRs were the only examples to carry MCW bodywork, this example entering service in February 1975. The full quota of 200 buses entered service between 1972 and 1976. *Malcolm Keeley*

A brand-new and gleaming East Midland Series 2 VRT, D105 (HAL 105K), stands resplendent in its dark red and ivory livery at Eastern Coach Works prior to delivery to the company. It entered service in November 1971.
MB Transport Photos

A variety of buses were specially painted to commemorate HM The Queen's Silver Jubilee in 1977, including a number of NBC VRTs. One of these was Southdown 565 (GNJ 565N), seen in silver livery with a light blue band and sponsored by Wadham Stringer.
Mark Hughes

An early example of ECW's revised front end was Mansfield District's Series 2 VRT, B112 (PRR 112L) which entered service in December 1972. It is seen several years later displaying the latest style of NBC decals and is now minus the 'B' prefix to its fleet number. It will be recalled that Mansfield District had operated one of the VRSL prototypes just a few years previously. *Bristol Vintage Bus Group*

One of Alder Valley's coach-seated, ultra-low VRs is seen at the Hillingdon Show in July 1976. The high-backed seats of 930 (HPK 507N) can be seen clearly in this view. At the time of writing this bus was an open-topper owned by SS Suncruises of Scarborough and used on that firm's seasonal seafront service, which operates alongside other VRs run by Scarborough & District. *David Brown*

5. THE ULTIMATE VR — SERIES 3

Unlike the Series 1, introduced straight from the drawing board, and the Series 2, which both upgraded and corrected previous problems and weaknesses found in the light of operating experience, the Series 3 VR not only featured further refinements but also introduced the final and most successful development in the VR series. A great deal of thought and development went into the Series 3, with a total of 3,052 being produced out of the 4,474 VRTs built. Two prototype chassis were constructed, the first being completed in November 1973 and the second during the following year, while Series 2 chassis were still in full production. In addition to these prototypes, Bristol also produced 12 pre-production chassis.

The first prototype entered service in the West of England with Western National during August 1974, while Northern General, based at the opposite end of the country, in the North East, received the second bus six months later, in February 1975. Western National was the first to try out the new Leyland 510 engine, from the 500-series range, in a VR, introduced as an option with Series 3 buses (see Appendix IV). Each of the pre-production buses also featured this engine, while the prototype supplied to Northern General was the odd one out in being fitted with a Gardner 6LXB unit. The pre-production buses were split between just two operators, with six each going to Southdown and Hants & Dorset. These joined their respective fleets between February and September 1975. Deliveries of production buses followed straight on from these and began a run of over 3,000 buses which continued for the next six years until VR production ceased altogether in August 1981 in favour of the new Olympian. By the sheer volume built, these vehicles became commonplace throughout England and Wales for many years, operating from remote rural outstations as well as from depots in many towns and cities.

The first difference to catch the eye between the newly modified ECW bodies and those of the Series 2s was the slightly deeper grille on the front cowl and, later on, the absence of the usual BRISTOL VR badge on NBC vehicles. Continuing round the vehicle, there were other differences

along the sides and back. The large grilles at each side of the engine cover, together with the smaller apertures near the top of the rear panel, had disappeared, giving way to a fully enclosed engine compartment, complete with a tray beneath the engine, to minimise engine noise. Engine ventilation was now achieved by means of a large grille placed under the rearmost upper-deck offside window, which drew air in by means of a fan and ducting. Hot air was then expelled through another grille on the rear nearside corner between decks, being drawn out by suction as the bus travelled along. In the winter, the best seats on the bus were the bench seats at the rear of the lower deck on the nearside; behind these was the ducting along which the hot air travelled on its way out of the engine compartment, making this a good place not only to warm up but also to dry out in bad weather! Conversely, these seats were to be avoided on a hot summer's day!

▲ King's Lynn bus station plays host to Lincolnshire Road Car 1920 (MVL 130P) and Eastern Counties VR286 (VEX 286X) during July 1987. The former was still part of NBC but VR286 had been sold to its management a few months earlier, in February. This latter vehicle is painted in the 'Venetian blind' style of livery adopted by several NBC fleets for selected inter-urban services and has also been upgraded with coach seats for added passenger comfort.
Malcolm Keeley

The rear engine cover now included some simple mouldings to add a hint of character to what otherwise would have been a rather bland area of the bus, and the centre panel now featured a removable lower section. After an absence of more than 10 years, black window rubbers also made a return.

In addition to the ultra-low and full-height bodywork offered to customers by ECW, a further option was produced in the shape of a convertible-open-top body. It had long been traditional for operators to convert some of their elderly double-deckers to permanent (occasionally convertible) open-toppers for use on coastal services during the summer season and then to mothball them for the winter. ECW's solution offered an attractive alternative — to run convertible open-toppers as normal buses during the winter months and to remove the roofs for the summer season. This would not only give their passengers a comfortable ride on a modern bus instead of on the more traditional 'boneshaker' but also enable these to operate as one-man buses, particularly as conductors generally had been phased out and double-manning would increase costs. It would also enable a modest fleet reduction, as convertible buses could be better utilised during the summer school holidays for this seasonal work. Indeed, ECW had previously built convertible-open-top bodies on rear-entrance Bristol Lodekkas, a total of 35 being produced from 1956 to 1964 for Bristol Omnibus, Crosville and Brighton, Hove & District.

Fifty convertible VRs were built and entered service during the latter half of 1977 and early 1978. By far the largest customer was Southdown, which took 30, including 10 that featured dual doors and central staircases. South Wales received three, Western National 11 and Hants & Dorset six. These last six remained on the mainland for only just over a year, however, before being shipped to Southern Vectis on the Isle of Wight in exchange for the same number of standard vehicles. Hants & Dorset no longer required open-top buses at that time, as from May 1978 its former seasonal Sandbanks service had been run by Bournemouth Transport as an extension to the latter's summer open-top service from Christchurch Quay, using convertible Fleetlines. It is pleasing to record that, at the time of writing, most of these convertibles are still extant, many still giving rides along various seafronts during the summer. Not to be forgotten are the two convertible open-toppers produced by Alexander for Cardiff City Transport, one of which is still giving pleasure to many on sightseeing tours of Bath with the Bath Bus Company.

A couple of orders which are worthy of mention came from the Atomic Energy Research Establishment (AERE) at Harwell and from an overseas customer in the Netherlands. AERE staff transport has been a feature of this establishment for many years, as has the interest in its vehicles from enthusiasts. In 1977 and 1979 seven new ECW-bodied VRs were supplied to AERE, giving its staff the same quality of vehicle as that offered by the mainstream bus operators.

By contrast, the customised bus supplied to the Netherlands was for the Sijthoff Pers newspaper group for use as a mobile hospitality vehicle by its regional newspaper *Haagsche Courant* in The Hague. It was supplied in December 1979 and was built to normal right-hand-drive layout. Ultra-low ECW bodywork was specified, which also featured fully hinged opening windows and a kitchen. Minimising overall height was of paramount importance to give the bus as much locational versatility as possible, and to save a few more millimetres it was fitted with low-profile wheels and tyres. Since its arrival it has been lowered even further and is now exactly 4m high !

◀◀ From 1983 NBC's new local-coach livery, later nicknamed the 'Venetian blind' livery, began to appear in a number of fleets. The colours chosen were selected by the various operating companies, and quite a number of VRs could be seen painted in this style across the country in a wide variety of colour combinations. Such buses were often used on medium-to-long-distance inter-urban services and had usually had their seating upgraded to semi-coach standard. Southern National 1084 (LOD 724P) is painted in brown and yellow stripes and is parked at Taunton depot in September 1988 some six months after privatisation. *Mark Hughes*

◀ West Riding was an independent company until it sold out to the Transport Holding Co in 1968. It passed to the National Bus Company upon its formation in 1969 and remained in State ownership for 18 years until January 1987, when it once again joined the private sector. Series 3 VR 756 (NWR 506P) is pictured during NBC days at the Bullring, Wakefield, heading for Leeds in January 1980. *Martin Curtis*

East Lancs built the coachwork on this gleaming Burnley & Pendle VR, seen taking a break at Burnley bus station in July 1978. New in October 1976, this was one of 14 similar vehicles in the Burnley fleet. *Malcolm Keeley*

▲ Two additional coachbuilders were added to the VR fold to join the four whose distinctive products were already plying the highways and byways. These were Willowbrook and Alexander. Of these newcomers, Willowbrook received orders from Cardiff City Transport for 26 buses, from East Kent for 28 and from Northern General for 29, all these buses being built to single-door layout. Alexander's customers comprised Northampton Transport, which ordered 36 dual-door buses, Cardiff City Transport, with 71 single-door vehicles, and Tayside, which ordered dual-door bodywork for its 25 long-wheelbase VRTLL3 chassis. Both of these coachbuilders styled their body designs to fully incorporate the engine area and avoid having a separate bustle at the rear. Indeed, unlike Series 2 VRTs, no Series 3s featured bustles, although the buses supplied to Rhymney Valley by East Lancs were borderline cases, in that their design featured an indented rear window.

Northern Counties supplied a further 19 'Jumbo' dual-door bodies for Reading Transport on long-wheelbase VRTLL3 chassis and was also chosen to provide single-entrance coachwork for the 15 VRs destined for Cleveland Transit, a new convert to the VR. Four operators favoured East Lancs with orders for their new bodywork. Those built with single doors went to Burnley & Pendle, which had 14, Rhymney Valley, with three, and Lincoln which had seven long-wheelbase VRTLL3s as well as four standard-length vehicles. Northampton, however, opted for dual-door layout for its six buses. Once again, however, the lion's share — more than 2,760 buses — was bodied at Lowestoft by ECW.

The grand total of 3,052 Series 3 VRTs, comprising 3,001 VRTSL3 and 51 VRTLL3 chassis, included for the first time (other than in the VRLs) Leyland-engined chassis as well as the more numerous Gardner power units. Bodywork was supplied by ECW (2,769), Alexander (132), Willowbrook (83), East Lancs (34) and Northern Counties (34).

After a run of 13 years, production of Bristol VR chassis ceased during 1981. The very last, complete with an ECW coach-seated body, went to Stevenson's of Spath in October as its 49 (UVT 49X), while the penultimate chassis had the distinction of being the last to leave ECW on 26 October, destined for local NBC company Eastern Counties as VR294 (VEX 294X).

Confidence in the VR had grown progressively as operators found it to be a reliable and robust workhorse which met their needs very well. It's hard to keep a good thing secret, and during the Series 3's six-year production run the number of operators ordering these buses increased, as did quantities ordered. Below is the impressive list of customers which ran these fine buses. Some still do!

AERE, Harwell
Alder Valley
Bristol Omnibus
Burnley & Pendle
Cardiff
Cheltenham District
City of Oxford
Cleveland Transit

Extolling the virtues of a monthly Reading Rover, Reading Transport 36 (NDP 36R) was painted in an overall advertising livery of light blue when photographed in April 1978. Bodied by Northern Counties, this was one of the long-wheelbase Series 3 VRTLLs supplied during 1976. *Martin Curtis*

Yorkshire Woollen took delivery of RYG 389R in January 1977 as its 780. The bus was photographed arriving at Leeds bus station in October 1987 bearing subsequent fleet number 835 and the attractive livery of Verona green and buttermilk which it wore during the West Yorkshire PTE 'Metrobus' era. This livery was also carried by the VRs of West Riding, West Yorkshire Road Car and Yorkshire Traction that worked in the PTE area. *Graham Jones*

A bird's-eye view of Stephenson's convertible open-topper TNJ 998S as it journeys along Southend seafront towards Shoeburyness during the summer of 1993. This former Southdown bus clearly shows the revised seating layout and centre staircase of ECW's dual-door VRs. Note also the central periscope mirror at the front of the bus. *John Hypher*

Yorkshire Traction ultra-low 854 (OWE 854R) passes through Barnsley on a warm summer's day in July 1990. This company was privatised in January 1987, and the traditional-style fleetname on the side provides a pleasing post-privatisation touch. *Graham Jones*

New to West Yorkshire in poppy red as 1997 in March 1978, WWY 127S is seen 16 years later in York with a new number — 994 — and a new livery of green and cream. It now belonged to Yorkshire Rider and operated in the city under the fleetname 'Rider York'. The local Rider York logo on the side of the bus is a clever variation of the company logo seen on the front! *Mark Hughes*

Cardiff City Transport purchased a grand total of 117 VRs, which were bodied by three coachbuilders — ECW, Alexander and Willowbrook. No 309 (SWO 309S) proudly displays its Willowbrook badge above the radiator grille as it waits at Cardiff bus station before setting out for Ely in June 1981.
Malcolm Keeley

Convertible open-top 709 (UFX 859S) was one of six transferred to Southern Vectis from Hants & Dorset during early 1979 in exchange for six standard VRs. Although little more than a year old, they were repainted from poppy red to leaf green and white by Hants & Dorset before being shipped to the Isle of Wight. Pictured during its early days on the Island at Shanklin in October 1980, this bus would be exchanged again during 1983 for a closed-top VR from Bristol Omnibus, which required open-toppers for its Weston-super-Mare–Burnham-on-Sea open-top service. Numbered 8607 by Bristol, it moved to Bath during its first winter with the company. With roof in place these buses are 2in higher than their standard ECW-bodied sisters, as the removable top stands slightly proud of the upper-deck panelling. Regrettably this particular bus has now been scrapped as a result of fire damage sustained in 1992.
Malcolm Keeley

With City of Gloucester fleetnames and the city coat of arms, Cheltenham & Gloucester dual-door 5121 (REU 311S) works a Gloucester local service in August 1984. Cheltenham & Gloucester Omnibus Co was formed in September 1983 when it was separated from Bristol Omnibus. It was privatised three years later, in October 1986. *Malcolm Keeley*

VRs with Alexander coachwork were supplied to three municipal operators — Tayside, Cardiff and Northampton. No 59 (VRP 59S) was one of 36 ordered by Northampton and entered service in October 1977. This style of coachwork, with a peaked front dome and rounded rear, was an unusual combination, but the large and distinctive radiator grille was characteristic of all Alexander-bodied VRs. *Martin Curtis*

Looking splendid in lined-out Cardiff Corporation Tramways livery with shaded fleet number, Alexander-bodied 343 (WTG 343T) is seen at the Cardiff rally in June 1981, more than 30 years since the last trams ran in the city. Cardiff had by far the greatest number of Alexander-bodied VRs, taking 71 of the 132 built. *Malcolm Keeley*

The Atomic Energy Research Establishment (AERE) at Harwell was unusual in buying brand-new buses for staff transport and ran the only VRs ordered for this purpose. Two of the fleet of seven are seen loading workers at Harwell during September 1989 before starting their homeward journeys. *Martin Curtis*

Possibly the only VR ever to be officially launched by the breaking of a bottle of champagne was Bristol Omnibus 5134 (TWS 915T), captured at the exact second by the author outside the studios of BBC Radio Bristol in 1982 when the bus was launched as an overall advertisement for the radio station. It was painted light grey with red and black lettering, styled to resemble a large transistor radio complete with VHF aerial running along the length of the roof. *John Hypher*

Another view of Bristol Omnibus 5134 as it takes part in one of Radio Bristol's outside broadcasts in its home city during the summer of 1983. This bus was also used for the live transmission of *Morning West* during a morning peak journey, which included interviews with passengers and company staff as it travelled in service through the city. *John Hypher*

All of Cumberland's VRs were
fitted with ECW ultra-low
bodywork. Pictured just weeks
after the company was
acquired by Stagecoach,
421 (FAO 421V) is seen in
Whitehaven in red and
sandstone livery during
August 1987. More than 300
Series 2 and Series 3 VRs were
supplied with this type of
body. *Simon Butler*

The application of the red,
white and black livery of Wilts
& Dorset suits the lines of this
ECW-bodied Series 3 VRT very
well. No 3455 (KRU 855W)
was new to Hants & Dorset in
December 1980 and passed to
Wilts & Dorset in April 1983.
The company is one of the few
former NBC subsidiaries still
to remain independent.
Phil Davies

Seen running through Cardiff in April 1981 during its first few weeks in service is Rhymney Valley 84 (GHB 84W), with 76-seat East Lancs coachwork. The batch of three to which it belonged had the only East Lancs bodies built to four-bay configuration on VR chassis. *Martin Curtis*

Eastern National 3083 (STW 27W) has operated with four owners while remaining in the same fleet! It was purchased in February 1981, when Eastern National was part of the National Bus Company. A management buyout then took it into private hands in December 1986 but the comany was later sold to the Badgerline group, which eventually became FirstGroup. The bus is seen at Chelmsford bus station in November 2000 almost 20 years after joining the fleet, still going strong with its fourth owner! *John Hypher*

Relatively few long-wheelbase VRTLLs were built, and Lincoln City Transport was one of just four operators to order them. Built in 1981 and bodied by East Lancs, 40 (UFW 40W) was one of seven such 86-seaters in the Lincoln fleet. It was photographed when 10 years old in July 1991. *Martin Curtis*

6.   A SEA OF CHANGE

The movement of vehicles between NBC companies gained momentum during the early 1980s, and Bristol Omnibus was the recipient of VRs which started life with Southdown, East Midland, West Riding, London Country and United Auto. This dual-door Series 2, 5204 (WUF 532K), was formerly Southdown 532 and joined the Bristol City fleet during 1982. It is seen in Bristol during February 1984 bearing the pre-privatisation Citybus fleetname. *Mark Hughes*

When the VR was launched in 1966, the British bus industry had been settled into its then form for almost two decades. This comprised municipal operators, the British Electric Traction (BET) group, the Transport Holding Co (THC), the Scottish Bus Group (SBG), the Ulster Transport Authority (UTA), London Transport and a multitude of independent operators. But before VR production had got properly underway, the industry structure started to change. Under the provisions of the Transport Act 1968, the THC and BET groups were amalgamated in 1969 to become the National Bus Company (NBC), and in designated conurbations the municipal undertakings in those areas were formed into new Passenger Transport Executives (PTEs). Others followed in the mid-'Seventies, after which things settled down for a while until the Transport Act 1985, which brought about the privatisation and sell-off of the State-owned National Bus Company and Scottish Bus Group. This legislation also ▼ Company and Scottish Bus Group. This legislation also

included a requirement for municipally owned bus operations to be formed into self-standing limited companies which could then be sold off to the private sector. The publicly owned PTEs and London Transport were similarly required to be sold off.

Before sale, many NBC and Scottish Bus Group companies were broken down into small, saleable units, which in turn created a whole host of new identities and new liveries. London Transport was also divided into a number of separate operating units with individual identities, and Greater Manchester PTE was split into two separate undertakings ready for sale. Thus from the mid-'Eighties, when the first sell-offs took place, a new independently run industry started to emerge.

Some of the resultant sales were to management buy-outs, while others were bought and soon started to be formed into new groupings of varying sizes, both by former NBC managers and outside buyers. These new groups variously went through periods of sustained growth, rationalisation, sale or merger; along the way they bought out many of the previous management buy-outs, eventually settling down into the handful of large independent groups — principally First, Stagecoach and Arriva — which today account for a significant proportion of the industry. These, together with a number of smaller groups, stand-alone municipal fleets and thousands of independent operators of varying sizes now make up the British bus industry.

With all these changes, VRs which for the most part started life in corporate NBC, municipal or PTE liveries have worn coats of many other colours during their service lives, reflecting the various organisational and ownership changes in their respective areas of operation. These changes aside, however, differing vehicle requirements brought about by service reorganisations saw VRs being widely transferred between NBC fleets. Others withdrawn by municipal and PTE operators were also bought by NBC and, after privatisation, by its former subsidiaries. For example, some ex-Tayside VRTLLs found new homes with National Welsh as did a number of

National Welsh placed 19 former West Midlands PTE MCW-bodied Series 2 VRTs in service during 1982. Pictured here at Cardiff Castle in June 1983 when just nine years old is XR1970 (NOB 413M), new in April 1974 and previously 4413 in the WMPTE fleet. *Mark Hughes*

Tayside ran a fleet of 25 long-wheelbase Series 3 VRTLLs which entered service during February and March 1977. The majority of these were powered by Gardner 6LXB engines, but the last five were equipped with Leyland 501 power units. Just as SBG had done in the early 1970s with its Series 1s, Tayside disposed of these very young buses during the early 1980s, to such fleets as National Welsh, Burnley & Pendle and Lincoln, leaving Scotland once again without any VRs! National Welsh took the five Leyland-engined buses in 1981, and HR6577 (OSR 210R), formerly 210 in the Tayside fleet, is seen at Cardiff bus station in June 1982. *Mark Hughes*

Some of the MCW-bodied VRs from the West Midlands PTE fleet found new homes with National Welsh, South Wales and Wilts & Dorset. The last-named's 3466 (GOG 682N) is pictured in immaculate condition in Bournemouth town centre before setting out on its next trip to Canford Heath in October 1987. Fifteen of these buses were acquired by Wilts & Dorset during 1987, receiving fleet numbers 3461-75; some, including 3466, had already passed to National Welsh (and been on loan to Crosville) before their arrival in Dorset. *Phil Davies*

Crosville HVG935 (OWE 277K) is seen passing through Oswestry on its way to Ellesmere. This bus was new to Sheffield Corporation in July 1972 and passed to South Yorkshire PTE upon the latter's creation in 1974. It was one of six to be purchased by Crosville in 1980 when just eight years old. *Mark Hughes*

A name which reappeared ahead of the NBC privatisation process was North Western. This, however, had nothing in common with the former BET company and was formed in 1986 to embrace the Merseyside operations of Ribble. Drawlane bought the company in March 1988 and expanded its sphere of operation to include services in the Greater Manchester area. Drawlane, which also owned Crosville, decided to transfer operations on the latter's northern periphery to North Western and Bee Line in December 1989, before selling the residue to PMT. Pictured at Wigan in April 1991 is 558 (RMA 439V), which had been new to Crosville in April 1980. The livery is mainly red, with a triangle of dark blue. *Mark Hughes*

redundant MCW-bodied VRs from West Midlands PTE. Wilts & Dorset also took a quantity of these MCW-bodied buses, while Crosville and Maidstone & District received some former Sheffield East Lancs-bodied VRs. Indeed, Tayside followed in the footsteps of the Scottish Bus Group in prematurely getting rid of its 25 VRs. Among other recipients of these very youthful buses were the municipalities of Burnley & Pendle and Lincoln, which between them purchased over half of these five-year-old Alexander-bodied vehicles. And so once again Scotland became devoid of the VR! Surprisingly, however, both Lowland Scottish Omnibuses and Kelvin Central later operated small fleets of second- (or third-) hand VRs from south of the border and were very happy with them, thereby vindicating the type with SBG's successors. Indeed, the changing nature of

the industry over the past few decades created the right environment for the VRs to enjoy their glory days several times over, right to the present day.

United Counties upgrades

Other changes went much deeper than a coat of paint or a change of ownership on the vehicle registration document. In the early 'Eighties United Counties embarked on a unique and imaginative programme of rehabilitation for some of its early 10- to 12-year-old flat-fronted Series 1 and Series 2 VRs to give them a new lease of life. The results were very effective, as, when viewed from the front, the modified buses looked just like standard Series 3s. The work was carried out to such a high standard that it was only their registrations — G-, H-, J-

The '760 Project' is fully described in the text. This view shows United Counties Series 2 VRT 760 (VNV 760H) in service at Kettering in October 1970 when just five months old. Ten years further down the road this bus would be used as the project 'guinea pig' and...

...emerged from works looking like this in February 1981. It is seen in Wellingborough nine months later, in November, still looking like a brand-new bus. At a casual glance, this bus could easily have passed as a brand-new Series 3.
Both Roger Barton

or K-suffix — that made the casual observer realise that something didn't quite add up. The so-called '760 Project' involved a total of 15 buses rebuilt from 1981 to 1986, starting with 'guinea pig' bus number 760, an H-registered Series 2 which had its transformation completed in February 1981. Much of its bodywork ahead of the front axle was completely rebuilt to accommodate the curved windscreen and Series 3 front cowl as well as the slightly wider Series 3 upper-deck dome. Other modifications included the fitting of an air throttle and power-assisted steering which were welcomed by drivers (the author speaks from personal experience!) and a five-speed gearbox. At the same time, the front doors were also converted from electric to air operation. For internal comfort, an improved heating system as fitted to Series 3 buses was installed, complete with the small tell-tale air-intake grille behind the nearside rear wheel. The seats were also completely re-trimmed in orange moquette. At the rear, the centre engine cover was modified from its one-piece layout to the split arrangement of the Series 3.

The other 14 buses in the programme were similarly rebuilt as follows but did not receive five-speed gearboxes.

Series 1		Series 2	
750	March 1982	769	December 1982
751	October 1982	772	March 1983
752	December 1981	773	June 1983
753	May 1982	774	February 1984
754	August 1982	775	August 1983
755	September 1981	776	November 1983
		778	May 1986
		779	April 1984

The motive for the project had been twofold. On the one hand it had been noted by engineering staff that the bodywork generally on Series 1 and the early Series 2 VRs had been seriously deteriorating in several respects for some time and that major remedial action would need to be taken to keep these buses on the road. This situation was by no means unique to United Counties, and other companies also had to carry out substantial repairs, particularly to flooring and pillars to bring the bodies back up to standard. On the other hand,

drivers had become increasingly unhappy with the heavy steering and poor heating on these buses, and industrial action had meant that these buses were being sidelined. Again, this situation was not unique to the company.

Accident-damaged 760 was selected as a testbed, not only to address these problems but also to go one stage further and examine the feasibility and costs involved in upgrading this bus as closely as practicable to Series 3 specification. In practice, the conversion was far more complicated than at first envisaged, but the experience gained and the relatively low costs incurred made it worthwhile for the programme to continue. A further 12 buses had been converted by the end of 1983, but thereafter the programme slowed down considerably, with just three further vehicles being modified between 1984 and 1986. In view of the success of this project, it is surprising that none of the other NBC subsidiaries carried out similar work to their earlier VRs.

Open-top conversions

As we have already seen, the first open-top VRs were the 52 convertibles produced by ECW and Alexander in the period 1977-9. Up to this time, traditional open-top seaside buses comprised mainly AEC Regents, Leyland Titans and Bristol Ks and Lodekkas, which were later joined or replaced by rear-engined Daimler Fleetlines and Leyland Atlanteans.

Other than at London and Stratford-upon-Avon, inland open-top sightseeing tours were still a thing of the future and so it was along the Sussex, Isle of Wight, Dorset, Devon, Cornwall, Glamorgan and Dyfed coasts that the first open-top VRs were to be seen. Deregulation of bus services under the 1985 Transport Act paved the way for growth in leisure services in towns and cities, along the coasts and around tourist centres. Many of these new services took full advantage of the allure of open-top buses as well as the superior vantage-point offered from the upper deck, which has proved to be a winner with overseas tourists and our own visitors alike.

To meet demand in a growing market, more Atlanteans and Fleetlines lost their roofs, followed later by MCW Metrobuses, Leyland Olympians, Dennis Dominators and rear-engined Leyland Titans. VRs also played a major part and continue to do so. Over 80 closed-top VRs were converted during the 1980s

Just two months out of workshops after conversion to open-top is FDL 681V, seen picking up passengers at Shanklin Esplanade in June 2000. Although the bus remained owned by Southern Vectis and was painted in prewar-style apple green and cream, the seasonal 44 service between Shanklin and Sandown was sub-contracted to the Village Bus Company, with buses being supplied by Southern Vectis for the duration of the contract. An interesting feature to alert would-be (and possibly confused) passengers is the notice on the front roof dome!
John Hypher

▲ and 1990s, and these included both flat-fronted examples and the more recent Series 2s and 3s. The vast majority of these carried ECW bodies, but a number of Willowbrook bodies were converted for their new sightseeing role in London on the Original London Sightseeing Tour.

Former SBG Series 1 VRs were used in open-top guise by Alder Valley on its Marlow–Windsor riverside service and by United Auto along the seafront at Scarborough, while ex-Ribble flat-fronted VRs were used by Eastern Counties / Guide Friday at Norwich. Indeed, until the end of the 2001 summer season, East Yorkshire still used a former Midland General Series 1 at Scarborough, and despite their years, a pair of former York-West Yorkshire flat-fronted Series 2s see regular daily use by Guide Friday on its York tour.

Later Series 2 and Series 3 open-toppers have seen service on the Isle of Wight with Southern Vectis and Westbrook Travel, in York with Guide Friday, Jorvik, and Viking; at Scarborough with SS Suncruises, in Bath with Badgerline /

Guide Friday, Bath Bus Company and Ryan's, in London with London Coaches, at Skegness with Lincolnshire Road Car, at Clacton with Eastern National, at Rhyl with Crosville Wales / Arriva Cymru, at Southend with Stephenson's Coaches, at Southsea with Provincial, at Weymouth with Southern National and at Weston-super-Mare with Badgerline, as well as at many other locations. Some of these operators selected buses from their own fleets for conversion, while others purchased their VRs secondhand for this purpose. At the time of writing many of these services were still in the hands of VRs — enjoying continued glory days, despite being more than two decades old!

Of the 52 convertibles, many of these are still in service, but have moved to new operators and new areas where they continue to provide enjoyment for holidaymakers on sightseeing duties. Pastures new for former Southdown convertibles have included Ryan's at Bath, Hedingham Omnibuses at Clacton, Stagecoach Cumberland in the Lake District, Dart Pleasure Craft at Totnes, Stagecoach Western Scottish on the Isle of Bute, Stagecoach Fife at St Andrews, Stagecoach Inverness Traction at Inverness, Rubicon at Bristol and Coastal & Country Coaches at Whitby (although Stagecoach has now forsaken most — if not all — of the former Southdown convertibles for decapitated Leyland Titans and Olympians). Indeed, one even ventured overseas to work for Apple Tours of New York. South Wales and Western National convertibles have also popped up in Bath with Badgerline / Guide Friday and at Scarborough with East Yorkshire as well as remaining on home ground (in the case of the former Western National buses) with Southern National at Weymouth and with Stagecoach Devon at Torbay. Most of those which started life with Hants & Dorset continue their coastal services on the Isle of Wight with Southern Vectis / Westbrook Travel and in Bath with Badgerline / Guide Friday and the Bath Bus Company. One of the two former Cardiff Alexander-bodied convertibles can also be found with the Bath Bus Company, running alongside a significant number of other VRs in the city.

During 2001 Bath, York, Scarborough and Rhyl provided the largest concentrations of open-top VRs, and it seems likely that this will continue, at least for the time being.

Greener, cleaner VRs

Much has been made of air pollution in recent years and progress towards reducing pollution from road vehicles has come both from Europe, in the shape of new regulations and improved engine specifications, and from oil companies, with a range of 'greener' fuels. But the pioneer in the field of practical measures to clean up the emissions from older vehicles was Guide Friday, which in early 1993 modified a 1975 former Nottingham Leyland Atlantean AN68 to run on liquid petroleum gas (LPG). Since then it has adapted further buses to run on LPG, including its small fleet of open-top Bristol VRs which are used exclusively on the York Tour. These are all former York-West Yorkshire buses — Series 2s DWU 839H and FWT 956J and Series 3s WWR 417-20S. Modifications to their Gardner diesel engines included the fitting of a carburettor and ignition system and lowering the compression ratio. Additionally, new fuel lines were fitted and their diesel tanks removed and replaced by new multi-chamber gas tanks. In order to achieve adequate clearance from the ground, part of the floor was raised by 3in to accommodate the tanks. LPG produces cleaner engine exhaust than does diesel fuel, and reduces the amount of particulates and carbon monoxide expelled into the atmosphere.

During the mid-1990s Guide Friday was also involved in the conversion of several London Pride buses to LPG, including an MCW Metroliner and some Dennis Dominators. Its first 'outside job', however, was the conversion of two Badgerline VRs to LPG operation during early 1994. Badgerline had agreed to participate in an experiment funded by the Department of Transport and Avon County Council to test LPG-fuelled vehicles in service in Bath, where incidentally, Guide Friday and Badgerline jointly ran the Bath Tour. The buses concerned were Gardner-engined Series 3s 5508 (KOU 794P), a local bus since new, and 5614 (MUA 873P), which started life with West Riding. The experiment involved these buses' running on normal all-day city services from May/June 1994, and by all accounts their performance was better than before! After their withdrawal from service the following year, both were bought by Guide Friday in January 1996. They were loaned to Bournemouth Transport in February/March for evaluation, and, upon their return to Stratford-upon-Avon, MUA 873P was

converted to open-top (in April). KOU 794P was retained in closed-top form; during 2001 this bus was still based at Stratford, whereas MUA 873P was working with the other open-top VRs in York.

New owners

As VRs were withdrawn as a result of scheduled fleet-replacement programmes and became available on the second-hand market, they were snapped up by numerous small independent operators, both for service work and for use as school buses. They have continued to maintain a presence in towns and villages for many years and in turn have been replaced by newer VRs which were no longer required by the large operators. At one stage, for example, over 60 VRs were being used by independents on schools duties in the Bristol area alone! Many independents built up quite respectable-sized fleets of these buses, with some reaching as many as 25-45 vehicles, such as Johnson's of Hodthorpe, Rennie's of Dunfermline, Alpine of Llandudno and Hedingham Omnibuses in Essex. Indeed, each of these continues to run large numbers of VRs. Another notable (if short-lived) operator of VRs was Nottingham Omnibus, which ran a fleet of 40 on competitive services in the city during 1993/4; half of these comprised the fleet formerly operated by Kelvin Central and were painted

Bristol VRs were among the first buses selected for conversion to run on liquid petroleum gas (LPG), and even today Guide Friday's fleet of sightseeing VRs in York run on this fuel. Pictured in Bath during June 1994 is 5508 (KOU 794P), one of two Badgerline VRs converted to LPG by Guide Friday earlier in the year for trials in Bath initiated by Avon County Council and the Department of Transport; this was to test buses running on cleaner fuel in all-day service and compare the results with those of normal diesel-fuelled buses. Both were painted in green livery with black skirts and light blue between decks, together with 'The Clean Fuel Bus' slogan in place of the more usual advertisements. Above the skirting are the logos of (to the left of the badger) Avon County Council and (to the right) the Department of Transport. This bus continues in service today — still with its roof intact — with Guide Friday at Stratford-upon Avon. *Allan Macfarlane*

In the early 1990s a number of the former East Kent Willowbrook-bodied VRs were purchased by London Coaches for use on the Original London Sightseeing Tour. Some were converted to open-top while others retained their roofs for winter use and private hires. New as East Kent 7991, BW91 (TFN 991T) is seen at Victoria during its last days in London in June 1999, as a sales and staff base. *John Hypher*

During 1993 and 1994 Bournemouth's Yellow Buses was subjected to intense competition along its main corridors from BHT Buses, trading as Routemaster Bournemouth and using Routemasters as well as an assortment of rear-engined buses which included some ex-Bournemouth vehicles! To counteract this incursion Yellow Buses responded by assembling a dedicated fleet of 18 buses which included four ex-Yorkshire Traction VRs. No 536 (RWA 860R), with ultra-low ECW bodywork, joined Yellow Buses in February 1994 as part of this 'battle' fleet and was photographed in the town centre during its first week in service. Although BHT Buses ceased running in August 1994, the four VRs were retained until the following July. *John Hypher*

into NO livery before despatch, even running in Glasgow in this guise until all were ready to travel south together!

A few of the former NBC fleets, including East Yorkshire, Western National and Wilts & Dorset, still run sizeable fleets of VRs, while others continue to operate reduced numbers. During the NBC era, however, two companies, one of the largest and one of the smallest, managed to avoid owning any VRs, but this situation was reversed after privatisation! Midland Red's bus services were divided among four fleets which were privatised between 1986 and 1988. These were Midland Fox, Midland Red West, Midland Red North and Midland Red South, each of which later ran second-hand VRs. Midland Red South and Midland Red North, which later became Stagecoach Midland Red and Arriva Midlands North, ran their fleets for several years until withdrawing their last examples during 1999 and 2000 respectively. The smaller operator, Provincial, also acquired some second-hand VRs and still runs these on stage services, school runs and seasonal open-top services in Southsea. When one bears in mind that even the youngest VRs are now over 20 years old, it is a wonderful testimony to the type that, even today, one doesn't have to travel far to see examples at work.

Others have continued overseas in a variety of roles. Well over 200 VRTs (and a few VRL coaches) have gone abroad, to many European countries as well as to Australia, New Zealand, Africa, Central America, Canada and the USA. Some of these are with private owners or in use as promotional vehicles or charter buses, but many are highly visible as sightseeing buses — in Melbourne and Katoomba, New South Wales (Australia), in Auckland, Wellington and Dunedin (New Zealand), in Vancouver, Ottawa and Halifax (Canada), in Panama City (Panama) and in New York, Denver, Boston and San Diego (USA). At least one VR is also in use as a shuttle bus to the Disney complex in Orlando. Some of these buses have been modified and fitted additionally with offside doors, and some have had their original nearside doors removed and re-panelled with an additional window, giving them a somewhat unusual appearance. Worthy of mention too are the four VRs recently converted by Simon Munden to left-hand drive for service overseas. These unique vehicles are not, however, carrying sightseers but still remain in his Bristol yard

awaiting a purchaser after those who ordered their conversion failed to fulfil their obligations.

The last Bristols

There is a common belief that after a long and distinguished history the last chassis to be produced by Bristol Commercial Vehicles at Brislington was the VR. It may come as a surprise to learn that this was not the case and that other double-deck chassis continued to be built for a couple of years after the last VR had left the factory! Indeed, this other chassis type was built alongside the VR for a couple of years — but what was it?

Known initially as the B45, it was launched as the *Leyland* Olympian. It is certainly true to say that the VR was the last Bristol-badged chassis to be produced by the company, but the early Olympians were arguably Bristols carrying Leyland

Photographed at Showbus, Duxford, in September 1994, People's Provincial 520 (AHU 514V) was new in May 1980 as Bristol Omnibus 5137. At privatisation, the Provincial fleet comprised the former Gosport & Fareham operation and Hants & Dorset's Fareham depot. *Mark Hughes*

Prototype GGM 431D became No 29 in the fleet of Osborne, Tollesbury, when it was acquired during 1973 from Bristol Omnibus. This bus originally went to Central SMT for testing and returned to Bristol in May 1970. Together with fellow prototype HHW 933D, it was sold to Bristol Omnibus, where it was numbered C5000 and remained until its sale to Osborne's. Pictured at Colchester bus station in July 1979, it was eventually scrapped in 1991. *Malcolm Keeley*

badges. Indeed, despite the badging, many were even licensed as Bristols. The first B45 prototype was bodied by ECW during 1979 and looked very much like a squarer VR complete with curved VR front cowl. It was the second prototype, however, that took on the more familiar Olympian appearance with a completely re-styled and squarer front cowl. This bus was completed during 1980 and was used to launch the model before entering service with Ribble during the summer. In all, nine prototype B45s were built by Bristol, followed by a production run of 995 Olympians which included three-axle chassis for export. Leyland Bus was, of course, involved in each stage of development, and it is interesting that apart from NBC, a number of traditional Leyland customers and the Scottish Bus Group purchased the 'Bristol' Olympian. Coachwork for these chassis was produced by Alexander, ECW, East Lancs, Marshall, Northern Counties and Roe.

At the end of 1982 NBC sold its share of Bus Manufacturers (Holdings) Ltd to Leyland, giving the latter sole control of both

Bristol and ECW. There quickly followed a policy of rationalisation, which spelled the end for Bristol within a year (and for ECW four years later). Sadly, therefore, the very last chassis to leave Bristol Commercial Vehicles did so in September 1983 destined for Devon General, its departure marking the end of an interesting and significant producer of quality bus, coach and lorry chassis. Production of the Olympian continued from Leyland's Workington plant. ECW survived a little longer but finally closed its doors in January 1987 after completing its last bus — an Olympian for London Transport. Thus another era ended and another great and distinguished name disappeared.

The Bristol legacy lives on, however, not least in the increasing number of VRs (as well as other models) entering preservation, and it is to be hoped that these will survive long-term for future generations to enjoy. I hope also that you, the reader, have enjoyed reading the story of the Bristol VR as much as I have enjoyed presenting it.

Western SMT's VRTs were delivered in a slightly darker red than normal. Inchinnan-based B2237 (NAG 588G) is seen in Renfrew during October 1970 on the 24 Glasgow–Renfrew–Paisley (Gallowhill) route, an early one-man-operated service. This bus was sold to Osborne's of Tollesbury, Essex, in 1973 and thus did not take part in the SBG/NBC exchanges. *Iain MacGregor*

Central SMT had 20 VRTs split between Wishaw depot in Lanarkshire and Old Kilpatrick (Gavinburn) in Dunbartonshire. Based at Gavinburn, BN357 (NGM 157G) is seen on a local service in Dumbarton during March 1970. It joined the Eastern Counties fleet during 1973. *Iain MacGregor*

◄◄ Alexander (Midland) MRT5 (SMS 35H) stands in Perth city centre on the trunk service between Cherrybank and Scone during July 1970. Midland had 15 VRTs, and these were the first to go (within 18 months of arrival) in the NBC exchanges, all passing in 1971 to Eastern National, where they initially retained their Midland blue livery. *Iain MacGregor*

◄ Scotland's first Bristol VRTs were of the 33ft-long variety and were used on the heavily loaded Glasgow city service to Easterhouse. Scottish Omnibuses AA282 (LFS 282F), photographed when just a few months old in February 1969, passed to Southdown in 1973. *Iain MacGregor*

The second batch of VRTs for Scottish Omnibuses were conventional 30ft models. This one passed to United Automobile Services and was later converted to open-top for use on the Scarborough seafront service. No 637 (OSF 310G) loads at North Bay, Scarborough, in July 1983. *Iain MacGregor*

Eastern National 3002 (CPU 981G) was among the earliest VRTs to enter service, in April 1969. Although in coach livery for the X10 Southend–London service, this vehicle was in fact fitted with bus seats and is seen travelling along Brighton seafront during May 1971. *David Brown*

Midland General 316 (BNU 680G) was delivered in the company's attractive blue and cream livery but when photographed at Nottingham in April 1974 had fallen victim to NBC poppy red. *BaMMOT collection*

Southdown 2095 (OCD 765G) was one of a batch of 10 Series 1 VRs, all of which happily were delivered in BH&D's attractive red and cream livery style despite the company's takeover by Southdown. It is seen away from its normal seaside surroundings, at Oxford's Gloucester Green bus station while on loan to City of Oxford in May 1971. *Malcolm Keeley*

Southdown Series 2 VRT 501 (SCD 501H) makes a splendid sight as it travels through Brighton in June 1971 in traditional Southdown livery when just a year old. It is pleasing that a number of traditional liveries were applied to some of the early VRs before 'corporatisation' consigned them to the history books. *David Brown*

Another traditional livery to grace the VR before 'corporatisation' completely took over was that of Devon General. Displaying something of a mix and match of old and new fleetnames, 542 (VOD 542K) heads towards Brixham in June 1974. *Mark Hughes*

In a simplified version of City of Oxford's unique livery, 901 (OFC 901H) leaves Gloucester Green bus station in Oxford bound for Aylesbury in May 1971. Entering service in April 1970, this was the very first Series 2 VRT and in later years was converted to open-top by the company. *Malcolm Keeley*

A picture of the way it used to be in Tilling green and cream together with the old-style gold fleetnames is Southern Vectis 628 (SDL 638J) heading towards Ryde through Godshill in August 1991, some 20 years after entering service on the Island. *Malcolm Keeley*

Sheffield Transport took delivery of 18 of these East Lancs-bodied Series 2 VRTs during the summer of 1972. No 269 (OWE 269K) is seen in Sheffield during April 1975 in the ownership of the South Yorkshire PTE, to which the Sheffield undertaking had been transferred during the previous year. *Mark Hughes*

Resplendent in traditional livery, Ribble's first VRT, 1979 (NCK 979J), leaves Talbot Road bus station, Blackpool, in July 1971, when just two months old. The company was no stranger to the VR, however, as it had run a VRL double-deck coach on Standerwick's London motorway service from the end of 1968, and earlier in 1971 had added a further 11 to the fleet. *Mark Hughes*

Locally based Metro-Cammell was chosen by West Midlands PTE as the coachbuilder for its sizeable order for 200 Bristol VRTs. In many respects, the body design of these buses was outwardly similar to that of other rear-engined double-deckers in the PTE fleet at the time. No 4372 (NOB 372M) is seen at Wednesbury bus station in July 1982.
Malcolm Keeley

Former BET subsidiary North Western Road Car Co ordered 25 ECW-bodied Series 2 VRTs, but in March 1972 part of this company was absorbed by the SELNEC (South East Lancashire North East Cheshire) PTE, which took over the order. The first of these, 400 (AJA 400L), was photographed at Altrincham during May 1973 when just five months old and still awaiting its owner's decals.
Mark Hughes

Eastern Counties Series 2 VRT VR158 (JNG 56N) is pictured by the Castle in Norwich while running on the local University service during 1976.
John Hypher

Eastern Coach Works produced its first full-height VR bodies towards the end of the production of Series 2 VRTs. The first and only customer to have these bodies mounted on Series 2 chassis was Maidstone & District, which received a total of 15 in July 1975. No 5742 (KKE 742N) was painted in this special livery to celebrate the Queen's Silver Jubilee in 1977 and was photographed in April of that year. Together with several other operators, M&D received further full-height bodies on Series 3 chassis from August 1975. *Mark Hughes*

Hutchings & Cornelius of South Petherton in Somerset was the first independent operator to purchase a new Bristol VRT. New in June 1973, RYA 700L works its way through Yeovil in January 1977. *Mark Hughes*

East Yorkshire's first VRs, which entered service during January 1973, were early recipients of the redesigned ECW bodywork with curved windscreens. They were delivered in the company's traditional blue livery but with white in place of primrose and with corporate (white) NBC fleetnames. No 928 (DKH 928L) was photographed in March 1974 at Hull in its distinctive colours. Upon repaint these buses emerged in poppy red. *Mark Hughes*

Merseyside PTE was the only operator to order the long-wheelbase, high-framed VRTLH chassis. Its order called for 60 of these vehicles but it received only 59 as one was destroyed by fire at bodybuilder East Lancs's factory. These buses' 80-seat dual-door bodywork featured an engine 'bustle' at the rear, as shown clearly in this April 1975 view of 2064 (YKF 702K).
Mark Hughes

Of the 30 Standerwick ECW-bodied VRLLH double-deck coaches, all but the last two were painted in Standerwick's red and cream livery. No 78 (PRN 78K), pictured at Preston bus station when brand new in August 1972, was painted in National white with light blue relief, while the last coach of the order, 79, was painted in all-over National white. The areas of blue break up the large area of white very nicely and present a pleasing and well balanced livery.
Mark Hughes

Brand-new Western Welsh HR1677 (SKG 895S) waits to return to Maerdy from Cardiff bus station in September 1977. Powered by an 8.2-litre Leyland 501 engine rated at 170bhp, it was only the second VR to be purchased by the company, which in 1978 would be merged with Red &White to form National Welsh. *John Hypher*

The only export of a new VR to Europe was an ECW-bodied ultra-low Series 3 VRTSL which was purchased by Sijthoff Pers, publisher of the Haagsche Courant regional newspaper in The Hague. Its coachwork was extensively customised by ECW for its use as a promotional and hospitality vehicle, and included a kitchen area at the lower rear and outward-opening windows on the UK nearside on both decks and at the front of the upper deck. The bus was delivered in December 1979 and remains in regular use today — still with the same driver! *Haagsche Courant*

Western National 1197 (LFJ 841W) boards the Torpoint Ferry on its journey from Plymouth to Cremyll. VRs regularly use this chain ferry, similar in operation to the Sandbanks Ferry which crosses the mouth of Poole Harbour and which is used by Wilts & Dorset's Swanage service. *John Hypher*

Lincolnshire Road Car 1949 (LVL 804V) makes a fine sight in the sunshine at Grimsby bus station during September 1995. Notice that the two upper-deck front windows have been reglazed without the usual outward-opening ventilators. *Mark Hughes*

Among the last handful of closed-top Bristol VRs with Arriva Cymru was DVG524 (BMA 524W), seen at Aberystwyth during July 2000. New in July 1981 to Crosville, when the company split in August 1986 DVG524 became part of Crosville Wales and remained in the fleet to be taken over by Arriva. *John Hypher*

Northern Counties supplied the bodywork for the 15 VRs in the Cleveland Transit fleet. No H112 (RDC 112R) is seen in Stockton during June 1980. *Malcolm Keeley*

Great Yarmouth operated 16 Series 3 VRs with bodywork built by Eastern Coach Works at Lowestoft, just a short distance away. New in February 1977, 32 (RVF 32R) was photographed on a local Yarmouth service in July 1979. These vehicles, together with the undertaking, later passed to Eastern Counties. *Malcolm Keeley*

Still going strong in July 2000 after 20 years of service in South Wales was First Cymru 980 (BEP 980V), seen leaving Swansea bus station bound for Brynamman. *John Hypher*

Some 220 full-height ECW bodies were built on VRTs for eight operators. Of these, 15 were ordered by London Country and became BT1-15, entering service during June / July 1977. BT1 (PPH 461R) is seen in January 1981 at the Lawrence Hill depot of Bristol Omnibus, which had acquired the whole batch after just 3½ years! *Mark Hughes*

In 1978 and 1980 Mayne's of Manchester purchased a total of five Series 3 VRs with coach-seated ECW bodies. No 17 (VJA 667S) passes through Manchester Piccadilly during July 1987 in Mayne's striking livery. *Mark Hughes*

▲ Pictured on the rally field at Duxford in September 2000 is former Trent 837 (BRC 837T), which dates back to February 1979. The high standard of finish to its paintwork is reminiscent of what the bus would have looked like when brand new! *John Hypher*

A magnificent paint job, showing what might have been if Aldershot & District had purchased VRs (albeit Series 1s). Alder Valley 611 (GGM 81W), resplendent in the attractive Aldershot & District colours, is shown to maximum advantage in the sunshine at the Southsea Spectacular in June 1981. *Malcolm Keeley*

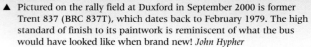

Another independent operator to order the VR was Stevenson's of Spath, which took a pair of ECW-bodied coach-seated examples. No 50 (PFA 50W) was new in November 1980 and is seen in Carrs Lane, Birmingham in July 1981. The proclamation between decks would have had to be altered three months later, when its second VR coach, 49, entered service. No 49 had the very last VR chassis built. *Malcolm Keeley*

Painted in Tyne & Wear PTE yellow is brand-new coach-seated United Automobile 816 (APT 816W), seen at Heddon in August 1980. These colours were applied to United Auto and Northern General buses which ran in the PTE area. *David Brown*

Pictured in April 1986 at Newcastle Haymarket is United Automobile 808 (APT 808W) in 'Venetian blind' livery. It had been re-seated with coach seats for use on the Tynelink service. *Mark Hughes*

One of Tayside Regional Council's short-lived long-wheelbase VRTLLs with bodywork by Alexander awaits departure for Whitfield in April 1977. No 205 (OSR 205R) was only two months old when photographed and was one of five which passed to Burnley & Pendle Joint Transport in 1982. *Stewart J. Brown*

VRs have carried their fair share of overall advertising liveries, which have come in a wide spectrum of colours and designs. Western National 1117 (VDV 117S) travels through Plymouth in September 1981 in overall black as one of several NBC VRs to carry the John Hill message. *Geoff Rixon*

Still in Luton Bus red in March 2000 was The Shires 5046, seen at Dallow Road, Luton. Luton & District had been formed in January 1986 from part of United Counties and was purchased in August 1987 by its employees. Relaunched as The Shires in subsequent British Bus ownership, the company is now part of the Arriva group.
John Hypher

Lincoln City Transport ordered 10 of these Series 3 VRTs with full-height ECW bodies. No 29 (RFE 29R) is seen at Lincoln bus station in July 1988 followed by long-wheelbase VRTLL 35 (NFW 35V) with East Lancs bodywork.
Mark Hughes

Midland Red was one of only two bus-operating NBC subsidiaries never to run VRs. After privatisation, however, each of Midland Red's four bus-operating successors remedied this situation. Pictured at Oswestry bus station in May 1993 is Midland Red North 1819 (YMB 519W), which was transferred from Crosville Wales in 1991.
Malcolm Keeley

Western National convertible open-topper 943 (VDV 143S) *Ark Royal* waits in Falmouth before setting out for Pendennis Point in September 1982. It was one of a batch of 11, all of which were painted in this livery, irrespective of whether they ran in Cornwall or Torbay. (Western National was a green fleet whereas Devon General was red.) New in March 1978, this bus remains active on the Badgerline / Guide Friday tour of Bath some 23 years later! *Geoff Rixon*

Before joining the Guide Friday fleet in 1996, MUA 873P had already worked for a number of operators since delivery to West Riding in November 1975. 'Cascaded' to Bristol Omnibus in May 1983, it passed to Badgerline in January 1986 and was transferred to Western National during November 1989. April 1993 saw it move back to Badgerline, where it was later converted to run on LPG by Guide Friday for a clean-fuel experiment in Bath, which commenced during the summer of 1994. Upon withdrawal it was sold to Guide Friday, which removed the roof for sightseeing work. Pictured at the Merchant Adventurers' House, York, in August 2000, the bus still runs on LPG, as do the other VRs on the York Tour. *John Hypher*

Among the VRs used by Bath Bus Company on its sightseeing tour of the city is convertible open-topper WTG 360T, one of a pair of convertibles purchased by Cardiff City Transport. Bodied by Alexander, it was new in February 1979. Still looking good, it was photographed near Bath Abbey over 20 years later, in September 2000. *John Hypher*

Arriva Cymru OVG528 (DCA 528X) was one of the small fleet of open-top VRs running in the Rhyl area during the 2000 summer season, all carrying this yellow, white and blue livery and 'Happy Dragon' brand-name. This bus was new to Crosville in August 1981 as DVG528 and was among the last VRs to be built. When the company was split in August 1986, it passed to Crosville Wales, which later converted it to open-top. Rhyl seafront was the setting for this photograph taken in July 2000.
John Hypher

Former Western National Series 2 VR 1081 (GTA 51N) is now owned by Westbrook Travel on the Isle of Wight and is used on circular sightseeing route 88 from Ryde via Sandown and places of local interest. It is pictured starting another tour from Ryde in June 2000, by which time it had clocked up more than a quarter of a century of service.
John Hypher

Showing off its immaculate Stagecoach livery in the late-morning sun at Bedford bus station is United Counties 939 (URP 939W), setting out for Biggleswade in March 2000.
John Hypher

Carter's of Colchester is the proud owner of this unusual bus with an interesting history. CBV 9S started out as a standard ECW-bodied double-decker with Ribble (2009) in August 1977. Upon withdrawal it moved south to Milton Keynes City Bus (3009) in May 1993 and, after spending time with Buckinghamshire Road Car and MK Metro, was withdrawn by the latter in January 1997 after sustaining severe roof damage. A couple of months later it was acquired by Guide Friday, which rebuilt it as a 30-seat single-decker which entered service in February 1998. Based in Stratford-upon-Avon, it was used on the Cotswold Tour and before leaving the company was re-registered HNP 165S. Carter's purchased this unique bus during the early months of 2001 and had it repainted into this smart red and yellow livery during the summer complete with fleet number VRS165. Currently with seating for 31, this is the only VR ever to operate in the UK as a single-decker, and Carter's intends to retain it for the foreseeable future.
John Hypher

Several VRs now carry First's 'Barbie 2' livery. The first to be outshopped in these colours was Western National 1197 (LFJ 841W), seen in Plymouth during May 2001 with paint barely dry. Further Western National VRs have now also received this treatment. *Graham Jones*

Making an early public appearance was United Counties 849 (OVV 849R) decked out in the attractively redesigned Stagecoach corporate colours. Seen at the North Weald bus rally in June 2001, 849 remains the only VR to carry this livery and is used as a group promotional vehicle. *John Hypher*

Ten Scottish Bus Group VRs went to Lincolnshire Road Car during the bus exchanges in 1973. No 1985 (NAG 592G) was formerly B2241 in the Western SMT fleet and is seen smartly turned out at Lincoln bus station in June 1983. Notice how much difference the black window rubbers make to the appearance of this bus. *Graham Jones*

Operator	Fleet No	Reg No	Type	To
Scottish Omnibuses	AA280	LFS 280F	VRTLL6G	Eastern Counties (VR307)
Scottish Omnibuses	AA281	LFS 281F	VRTLL6G	Eastern Counties (VR309)
Scottish Omnibuses	AA282	LFS 282F	VRTLL6G	Southdown (542)
Scottish Omnibuses	AA283	LFS 283F	VRTLL6G	Eastern Counties (VR312)
Scottish Omnibuses	AA284	LFS 284F	VRTLL6G	Alder Valley (893)
Scottish Omnibuses	AA285	LFS 285F	VRTLL6G	Alder Valley (894)
Scottish Omnibuses	AA286	LFS 286F	VRTLL6G	Eastern Counties (VR311)
Scottish Omnibuses	AA287	LFS 287F	VRTLL6G	Eastern National (3042)
Scottish Omnibuses	AA288	LFS 288F	VRTLL6G	Southdown (549)
Scottish Omnibuses	AA289	LFS 289F	VRTLL6G	Southdown (543)
Scottish Omnibuses	AA290	LFS 290F	VRTLL6G	Eastern Counties (VR306)
Scottish Omnibuses	AA291	LFS 291F	VRTLL6G	Eastern Counties (VR301)
Scottish Omnibuses	AA292	LFS 292F	VRTLL6G	Eastern National (3043)
Scottish Omnibuses	AA293	LFS 293F	VRTLL6G	Eastern Counties (VR304)
Scottish Omnibuses	AA294	LFS 294F	VRTLL6G	Eastern Counties (VR305)
Scottish Omnibuses	AA295	LFS 295F	VRTLL6G	Eastern National (3044)
Scottish Omnibuses	AA296	LFS 296F	VRTLL6G	Southdown (544)
Scottish Omnibuses	AA297	LFS 297F	VRTLL6G	Southdown (545)
Scottish Omnibuses	AA298	LFS 298F	VRTLL6G	Southdown (546)
Scottish Omnibuses	AA299	LFS 299F	VRTLL6G	Southdown (547)
Scottish Omnibuses	AA300	LFS 300F	VRTLL6G	Southdown (548)
Scottish Omnibuses	AA301	LFS 301F	VRTLL6G	Eastern Counties (VR308)
Scottish Omnibuses	AA302	LFS 302F	VRTLL6G	Eastern Counties (VR310)
Scottish Omnibuses	AA303	LFS 303F	VRTLL6G	Eastern Counties (VR303)
Scottish Omnibuses	AA304	LFS 304F	VRTLL6G	Eastern Counties (VR302)
Scottish Omnibuses	AA305	OSF 305G	VRTSL6G	Southern Vectis (620)
Scottish Omnibuses	AA306	OSF 306G	VRTSL6G	Eastern Counties (VR324)
Scottish Omnibuses	AA307	OSF 307G	VRTSL6G	Southern Vectis (621)
Scottish Omnibuses	AA308	OSF 308G	VRTSL6G	Eastern Counties (VR325)
Scottish Omnibuses	AA309	OSF 309G	VRTSL6G	Eastern Counties (VR326)
Scottish Omnibuses	AA310	OSF 310G	VRTSL6G	United Auto (637)
Scottish Omnibuses	AA311	OSF 311G	VRTSL6G	United Auto (638)
Scottish Omnibuses	AA312	OSF 312G	VRTSL6G	United Auto (639)
Scottish Omnibuses	AA313	OSF 313G	VRTSL6G	United Auto (640)
Scottish Omnibuses	AA314	OSF 314G	VRTSL6G	United Auto (641)
Central SMT	BN357	NGM 157G	VRTSL6G	Eastern Counties (VR316)
Central SMT	BN358	NGM 158G	VRTSL6G	Alder Valley (881)
Central SMT	BN359	NGM 159G	VRTSL6G	Alder Valley (882)
Central SMT	BN360	NGM 160G	VRTSL6G	Alder Valley (883)
Central SMT	BN361	NGM 161G	VRTSL6G	Alder Valley (884)
Central SMT	BN362	NGM 162G	VRTSL6G	Eastern Counties (VR320)
Central SMT	BN363	NGM 163G	VRTSL6G	Lincolnshire (1980)
Central SMT	BN364	NGM 164G	VRTSL6G	Eastern Counties (VR327)
Central SMT	BN365	NGM 165G	VRTSL6G	Eastern Counties (VR323)
Central SMT	BN366	NGM 166G	VRTSL6G	Eastern Counties (VR322)
Central SMT	BN367	NGM 167G	VRTSL6G	Lincolnshire (1981)
Central SMT	BN368	NGM 168G	VRTSL6G	Southern Vectis (619)
Central SMT	BN369	NGM 169G	VRTSL6G	Lincolnshire (1982)
Central SMT	BN370	NGM 170G	VRTSL6G	Eastern Counties (VR321)
Central SMT	BN371	NGM 171G	VRTSL6G	Lincolnshire (1983)
Central SMT	BN372	NGM 172G	VRTSL6G	United Auto (634)
Central SMT	BN373	NGM 173G	VRTSL6G	Lincolnshire (1984)
Central SMT	BN374	NGM 174G	VRTSL6G	Eastern Counties (VR319)

Southern Vectis took three ex-SBG VRs, comprising a pair from Scottish Omnibuses and a single bus from Central SMT. No 621 (OSF 307G) came from Scottish Omnibuses, where it had been numbered AA307. Looking smart during October 1980 after a recent repaint, it had received an English-style destination display while on the Island. New in June 1969, and now more than 30 years old, this bus is still in the fleet of Johnson's of Hodthorpe at the time of writing. *Malcolm Keeley*

Operator	Fleet No	Reg No	Type	To
Central SMT	BN375	NGM 175G	VRTSL6G	United Auto (635)
Central SMT	BN376	NGM 176G	VRTSL6G	United Auto (636)
Western SMT	B2262	NAG 583G	VRTSL6G	Eastern National (3045)
Western SMT	B2263	NAG 584G	VRTSL6G	Eastern Counties (VR333)
Western SMT	B2264	NAG 585G	VRTSL6G	Eastern Counties (VR330)
Western SMT	B2265	NAG 586G	VRTSL6G	Eastern National (3046)
Western SMT	B2236	NAG 587G	VRTSL6G	Eastern Counties (VR332)
Western SMT	B2237	NAG 588G	VRTSL6G	Osborne, Tollesbury (26)
Western SMT	B2238	NAG 589G	VRTSL6G	Eastern Counties (VR331)
Western SMT	B2239	NAG 590G	VRTSL6G	Alder Valley (885)
Western SMT	B2240	NAG 591G	VRTSL6G	Eastern Counties (VR328)
Western SMT	B2241	NAG 592G	VRTSL6G	Lincolnshire (1985)
Western SMT	B2242	NCS 435G	VRTSL6G	Lincolnshire (1986)
Western SMT	B2243	NCS 436G	VRTSL6G	Lincolnshire (1987)
Western SMT	B2244	NCS 437G	VRTSL6G	Lincolnshire (1988)
Western SMT	B2245	OCS 575H	VRTSL6G	Lincolnshire (1989)
Western SMT	B2246	OCS 576H	VRTSL6G	Eastern National (3047)
Western SMT	B2247	OCS 577H	VRTSL6G	Richardsons, Oldbury
Western SMT	B2248	OCS 578H	VRTSL6G	Eastern Counties (VR318)
Western SMT	B2249	OCS 579H	VRTSL6G	Eastern Counties (VR317)
Western SMT	B2250	OCS 580H	VRTSL6G	Eastern Counties (VR329)
Western SMT	B2251	OCS 581H	VRTSL6G	Osborne, Tollesbury (27)
Western SMT	B2252	OCS 582H	VRTSL6G	United Auto (642)
Western SMT	B2253	OCS 583H	VRTSL6G	United Auto (643)
Western SMT	B2254	OCS 584H	VRTSL6G	United Auto (644)
Western SMT	B2255	OCS 585H	VRTSL6G	United Auto (645)
Western SMT	B2256	OCS 586H	VRTSL6G	United Auto (646)
Western SMT	B2257	OCS 587H	VRTSL6G	United Auto (647)
Western SMT	B2258	OCS 588H	VRTSL6G	United Auto (648)
Western SMT	B2259	OCS 589H	VRTSL6G	United Auto (649)
Western SMT	B2260	OCS 590H	VRTSL6G	United Auto (650)
Western SMT	B2261	OCS 591H	VRTSL6G	United Auto (651)
Western SMT	B2266	OCS 592H	VRTSL6G	United Auto (652)
Western SMT	B2267	OCS 593H	VRTSL6G	United Auto (653)
Western SMT	B2268	OCS 594H	VRTSL6G	Alder Valley (886)
Western SMT	B2269	OCS 595H	VRTSL6G	Alder Valley (887)
Western SMT	B2270	OCS 596H	VRTSL6G	Alder Valley (888)
Western SMT	B2271	OCS 597H	VRTSL6G	Alder Valley (889)
Western SMT	B2272	OCS 598H	VRTSL6G	Alder Valley (890)
Western SMT	B2273	OCS 599H	VRTSL6G	Alder Valley (891)
Western SMT	B2274	OCS 600H	VRTSL6G	Alder Valley (892)
Alexander (Midland)	MRT1	SMS 31H	VRTSL6G	Eastern National (3005)
Alexander (Midland)	MRT2	SMS 32H	VRTSL6G	Eastern National (3006)
Alexander (Midland)	MRT3	SMS 33H	VRTSL6G	Eastern National (3007)
Alexander (Midland)	MRT4	SMS 34H	VRTSL6G	Eastern National (3008)
Alexander (Midland)	MRT5	SMS 35H	VRTSL6G	Eastern National (3009)
Alexander (Midland)	MRT6	SMS 36H	VRTSL6G	Eastern National (3010)
Alexander (Midland)	MRT7	SMS 37H	VRTSL6G	Eastern National (3011)
Alexander (Midland)	MRT8	SMS 38H	VRTSL6G	Eastern National (3012)
Alexander (Midland)	MRT9	SMS 39H	VRTSL6G	Eastern National (3013)
Alexander (Midland)	MRT10	SMS 40H	VRTSL6G	Eastern National (3014)
Alexander (Midland)	MRT11	SMS 41H	VRTSL6G	Eastern National (3015)
Alexander (Midland)	MRT12	SMS 42H	VRTSL6G	Eastern National (3016)
Alexander (Midland)	MRT13	SMS 43H	VRTSL6G	Eastern National (3017)
Alexander (Midland)	MRT14	SMS 44H	VRTSL6G	Eastern National (3018)
Alexander (Midland)	MRT15	SMS 45H	VRTSL6G	Eastern National (3019)

◄ Former Central SMT BN360 was one of 14 ex-SBG VRs to join the Alder Valley fleet in 1973. No 883 (NGM 160G) is seen at Windsor in June 1976 and still retains its Scottish-style destination arrangement. *Malcolm Keeley*

Eastern National received all 15 VRTs from Alexander (Midland) in 1971 in exchange for the same number of Lodekka FLF6Gs. No 3011 (SMS 37H) was photographed ◄ soon after acquisition at Victoria Coach Station prior to returning to Southend on the 400 service. This bus was originally numbered MRT7 in the Midland fleet. Notice the unusual small circular trafficators. *John Hypher*

By far the largest recipient of ex-Scottish VRTs was Eastern ◄ Counties, which took 12 former Scottish Omnibuses long-wheelbase VRTLLs and a total of 18 VRTSLs from Scottish Omnibuses, Central SMT and Western SMT. VR301 (LFS 291F) was one of the long-wheelbase buses to start a new life south of the border and was photographed at Norwich bus station during August 1980. *Malcolm Keeley*

APPENDIX II: VR CHASSIS AND BODY TOTALS

VRX prototypes and VRLs

Chassis	ECW	Bus Bodies (SA)	Total
VRX	2		2
VRLLH	1	25	26
VRLLH (Series 2)	29		29
Total	32	25	57

VRTs

Chassis	ECW	East Lancs	Alexander	Willowbrook	N Counties	MCW	(not bodied)	Total
VRTLL	25							25
VRTSL	227*						10*	237
VRTLL (Series 2)					31			31
VRTLH (Series 2)		59‡					1‡	60
VRTSL (Series 2)	798	68			3	200		1069
VRTLL3		7	25		19			51
VRTSL3	2769	27	107	83	15			3001
Total	3819	161	132	83	68	200	11	4474

Notes

* The 10 chassis at East Lancs were destroyed by fire together with any bodywork they may have received. However, one chassis was later salvaged and exported to Australia.

‡ One of the chassis together with any bodywork constructed was destroyed by fire at East Lancs.

Seven VRTSL chassis, comprising one Series 1 and six Series 3s, were rebodied by ECW as a result of fire or other damage. These were as follows:

Western SMT B2251 (OCS 581H)	1971
West Yorkshire 1715 (DWU 298T)	1979
Hants & Dorset 3424 (ELJ 216V)	1980
United Auto 803 (XPT 803V)	1980
South Wales 906 (OCY 906R)	1981
South Wales 959 (WTH 959T)	1981
East Kent 7655 (XJJ 655V)	1983

APPENDIX III: VRT CUSTOMER TOTALS

Western National	244
Crosville	243
Southdown	234
Eastern Counties	220
United Counties	218
United Auto	204
Bristol Omnibus / Cheltenham District	203
West Midlands PTE	200
West Yorkshire (including Keighley and York)	170
Maidstone & District	156
Hants & Dorset	150
Potteries	131
Thames Valley / Alder Valley	130
West Riding / Yorkshire Woollen	128
East Midland / Mansfield District	127
City of Cardiff Transport	117
Northern General	116
Trent / Midland General	111
Merseyside PTE	110
Eastern National	109
Yorkshire Traction	106
City of Oxford	97
South Wales	91
Ribble	83
East Yorkshire	79
East Kent	70
Lincolnshire	70
Southern Vectis	70
Red & White / Western Welsh / National Welsh	56
Reading Corporation/Transport	50
Northampton Transport	42
Western SMT	39
Cumberland	38
Stockport Corporation / SELNEC PTE	35
Scottish Omnibuses	35
Tayside Regional Transport	25
Burnley & Pendle Joint Transport	24
Lincoln City Transport	21
Central SMT	20
Sheffield Transport	18
Great Yarmouth Transport	16
Alexander Midland	15
Cleveland Transit	15
London Country	15
AERE, Harwell	7
Gelligaer UDC / Rhymney Valley DC	6
Mayne, Manchester	5
Stevenson's, Spath	2
Dept of Environment	1
Hutchings & Cornelius, South Petherton	1
Sijthoff Pers	1
Total	4,474

APPENDIX IV:
CHASSIS AND BODY SPECIFICATIONS

Chassis designations

The first three letters relate to the engine position:

VRL   Vertical Rear Longitudinal (offside corner of chassis)

VRT   Vertical Rear Transverse (across back of chassis)

The fourth letter relates to the wheelbase:

L   Long wheelbase (18ft 6in)

S   Short wheelbase (16ft 2in)

The fifth letter relates to the frame height:

H   High frame (1ft 9½in in the area between the axles)

L   Low frame (1ft 6in in the area between the axles)

Dimensions

	VRX	VRLLH	VRTLL and VRTLH	VRTSL
Wheelbase	16ft 2in	18ft 6in	18ft 6in	16ft 2in
Overall length	32ft 7in	35ft 2½in	32ft 2½in*	30ft 5½in*
Overall width	8ft 2½in	8ft 2½in	8ft 2½in	8ft 2½in

* Series 1 VRT chassis were 1in shorter overall owing to a 1in shorter rear overhang.

Engine options

When first announced, the following engines were offered in the VR range:

Gardner 6LW	8.4 litres	112bhp @ 1,700rpm
Gardner 6LX	10.45 litres	150bhp @ 1,700rpm
Gardner 6LXB	10.45 litres	180bhp @ 1,850rpm
AEC AV691	11.3 litres	160bhp @ 1,900rpm
Leyland O.600	9.8 litres	125bhp @ 1,700rpm
Leyland O.680	11.1 litres	150bhp @ 2,000rpm

In practice, however, the only engines installed were the Gardner 6LX and 6LXB in all VRT variations in Series 1 and Series 2 form and the Leyland O.680 in all VRLLH chassis.

For Series 3 VRTs, the choice of Gardner 6LX and 6LXB engines was joined by the Leyland 500-series turbocharged 8.2-litre power unit developing 170bhp at 2,000rpm. Leyland 510 engines were fitted to prototype and pre-production Series 3s and the 501 variant to production models. The Gardner 6LX option was withdrawn in 1976.

During the latter part of 1980 a disruption in the supply of 6LXB engines from Gardner was met with the offer of some examples of the new 6LXC engine, normally derated to 180bhp, while Bristol Commercial Vehicles (BCV) was able to obtain more Leyland 501 engines; these were offered to customers if deliveries were to be maintained on schedule. BCV also obtained a supply of Leyland O.680 engines which were accepted by two customers (Southdown and Bristol Omnibus) and were the only examples fitted to VRT chassis.

Most of the 501 and O.680 engines were subsequently replaced by Gardner 6LX and 6LXB engines by their owners. Operators also replaced a number of 6LX and 6LXC engines with the 6LXB in the course of overhaul.

During 1986 Potteries 705 (GRF 705V) had its Leyland 501 engine replaced experimentally with a 10-litre Cummins L10 unit, which it would retain for the rest of its service life.

Transmission options

Fluid coupling (17¼in diameter) and Bristol / Self-Changing Gears four- or five-speed epicyclic gearbox with choice of:

CAV semi-automatic electro-pneumatic control

CAV fully-automatic control

Leyland G2 fully-automatic control

Leyland LVA45 fully-automatic control

Other specifications

Rear axle

Bristol double-reduction drop-centre, with differential between spiral and spur gears, a choice of final-drive ratios and a capacity of 10 tons.

Suspension

Semi-elliptic leaf springs.

Brakes

Dual-line split system full air, both axles with spring parking brake on rear.

Tyres

10.00 x 20 14-ply on all wheels (not Series 3)

11R x 22.5 radials fitted on all wheels (Series 3)

ECW bodywork dimensions

Length

The standard ECW body fitted to the VRTLL was 32ft 9½in long.

The standard ECW body fitted to the VRTSL was 30ft 6½in long in original flat-screen form or 30ft 9in long with BET-style curved windscreen.

Height

Ultra-low	13ft 5in (special decambered springs)
Standard	13ft 8in
Convertible open-top	13ft 10in
Full-height	14ft 6in

The information in this appendix is based on material contained in *Chassis List C1408: Bristol VR Series*, published by the PSV Circle.

◀ **General Arrangement drawing of the Series 1 Bristol VRTSL chassis.** *Commercial Motor*

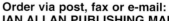
96 »